wisdom *of the* sadhu

TEACHINGS OF SUNDAR SINGH

compiled and edited by kim comer

D0646179

✈ PLOUGH PUBLISHING HOUSE

Published by Plough Publishing House
Walden, New York
Robertsbridge, England
Elsmore, Australia
www.plough.com

ISBN-10: 0-87486-998-6
ISBN-13: 978-0-87486-998-9

The editor gratefully acknowledges CLS Madras and the
Sadhu Sundar Singh Trust for permitting him to make free use
of previously published works by Sundar Singh.

A catalog record for this book is available
from the British Library

Library of Congress Cataloging-in-Publication Data
Singh, Sundar, 1889–
   Wisdom of the sadhu : teachings of Sundar Singh / compiled
& edited by Kim Comer.
      p. cm.
Includes bibliographical references.
   ISBN 0-87486-998-6 (alk. paper)
   1. Meditations. 1. Comer, Kim, 1962– 11. Title.
   bv4832.2 .s529 2000
   242–dc21   00-010387

wisdom of the sadhu

CONTENTS

Seek not to understand so that thou mayest believe, but believe so that thou mayest understand.

Augustine of Hippo

to the reader

As a large, red sun rises from the Punjabi plains, the solitary figure of a sadhu—an Indian holy man—comes into view, trudging along a dusty road. In another frame the figure appears again, this time toiling to reach a remote Tibetan village along a narrow, icy track better suited for goats than for humans. In yet another, the man appears at the edge of an ancient marketplace at dusk, mingling with the crowd as he seeks a place to sit and rest. Wherever this sadhu appears, those who look into his eyes immediately sense his extraordinary humility and peace. They discover a mystic...

Just as Sundar Singh appeared in such scenes again and again—without prior announcement, without introduction, without credentials—so he appears in this book. "Scenes," the first section, contains impressions from key events in his life. It is based both on accounts by Sundar Singh himself, and by writers who knew him. "Conversations," the second, contains dialogues that draw freely on material from all six of

Sundar Singh's books, as well as interviews and articles. Both sections are interspersed with parables that punctuate the themes. Though structurally unusual, the resulting collage allows us to encounter the sadhu in the way his contemporaries did: not as a systematic thinker, but as a personal teacher.

In his teachings as in his life, Sundar Singh offers little by way of rational orientation. He defies categorization and critical analysis. The impact of his message, however, is always direct and immediate. His voice rings with a clarity that rises from the deepest, clearest sources of life itself.

K. C.

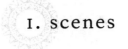 I. scenes

the hungry birds

Once as I wandered in the mountains, I came upon an outcropping of rocks, and as I sat on the highest rock to rest and look out over the valley, I saw a nest in the branches of a tree. The young birds in the nest were crying noisily. Then I saw how the mother bird returned with food for her young ones. When they heard the sound of her wings and felt her presence nearby, they cried all the more loudly and opened their beaks wide. But after the mother bird fed them and flew away again, they were quiet. Climbing down to look more closely, I saw that the newly hatched birds had not yet opened their eyes. Without even being able to see their mother, they opened their beaks and begged for nourishment whenever she approached.

These tiny birds did not say: "We will not open our beaks until we can see our mother clearly and also see what kind of food she offers. Perhaps it is not our mother at all but instead some dangerous enemy. And who knows if it is proper nourishment or some kind of poison that is being fed to us?" If they had reasoned thus, they would never have discovered the truth. Before they were even strong enough to open their eyes, they would have starved to death. But they held no such doubts about the presence and love of their mother, and so after a few days, they opened their eyes and rejoiced to see her with them. Day by day they grew stronger and developed into the form and likeness of the mother, and soon they were able to soar up into the freedom of the skies.

We humans often think of ourselves as the greatest living beings, but do we not have something to learn from these common birds? We often question the reality and the loving nature of God. But the Master has said: "Blessed are those who have not seen and yet believe." Whenever we open our hearts to God, we receive spiritual nourishment and grow more and more into the likeness of God until we reach spiritual maturity. And once we open our spiritual eyes and see God's presence, we find indescribable and unending bliss.

dharma · *devotion*

Candlelight flickers across the worn pages, and the Sanskrit characters dance rhythmically, like graceful maidens chanting ancient hymns. Transfixed, the young boy follows their motion, and his soul sings in unison with them:

> A mass of radiance, glowing all around,
> I see thee, hard to look at, on every side;
> Glory of flaming fire and sun, immeasurable,
> without beginning, middle, or end of power.
> Infinite arms, whose eyes are the moon and sun,
> I see thee, whose face is flaming fire,
> burning the whole universe with thy radiance.

Quietly another voice enters the song. It is a gentle, beloved voice, calling him, calling "Sundar," drawing him out of the chant, away from the dance. Slowly closing his inner eyes, he looks up into the candlelit face of his mother. "Come, Sundar! It is past midnight already. Soon it will be morning. You are only eight years old, my son. You must rest."

Obediently, reverently the boy returns the holy books to their place and seeks his mat. The candle flickers one last time and dies. Later he remembers:

Although my family was Sikh, we had great reverence for the Hindu scriptures. My mother was a living example of the love of God and a devoted follower of Hindu teachings. Every day she awoke before dawn, prepared herself with the cold water of the ritual bath, and read either from the *Bhagavad Gita* or from one of the other sacred writings. Her pure life and her complete devotion influenced me more strongly than it did the other family members. From the time of my earliest memories, she impressed upon me one rule above all others: when I woke from sleep, my first duty was to pray to God for spiritual nourishment and blessings. Only then could I break the night's fast. Sometimes I objected to this rule and insisted on having breakfast first, but my mother would never relent. Usually with coaxing, but when necessary with force, she impressed this rule deep onto my soul: Seek God first and only then turn to other things.

At that time, I was too young to recognize the true value of this education, and I resisted her. Later, however, I came to appreciate her example. Whenever I think back now on her loving guidance, I cannot thank

God enough for her. For she planted in me, and tended in my early life, a profound love and fear of God. She carried a great light within her, and her heart was the best spiritual training anyone could have: "You must not be careless and worldly," she would say. "Seek peace of soul, and love God always. Someday you must give yourself fully to the search, you must follow the way of the sadhu."

———

With pleading eyes, the boy looks up at his father:

Please help her, Father! She is so old and the weather is turning cold. I spent all my pocket money to buy food for her, but I did not have enough for a blanket. Please give me money to buy her a blanket.

Sardar Sher Singh retorts:

Listen, Sundar! Over the years I have given that widow all manner of help. We are not responsible for her. The other people in town should also help look after her. They must also learn charity. You cannot be responsible for everyone all the time. Others must learn to play their part. Do not worry about her now. You have done more than enough for her.

Downcast, the boy turns away. Agony of conscience.

Has not Mother always said we should show compassion and pity? Has Father no heart? What if no one else helps her? She might freeze in the night. Is there nothing I can do? Maybe...No, I mustn't! That would be wrong. But then again, Father has so much; he will never miss a few rupees. It is for a good cause; I'm not stealing for myself...

Sundar was wrong. Father does miss it. In the evening, Sardar Sher Singh calls together the household and announces that he is missing five rupees. "Has anyone taken money from my purse?" he asks, gently but firmly. Each one answers in turn. Sundar quietly says, "No Father, I didn't do it." The day closes somber and unresolved.

Sundar sleeps fitfully. He tosses and turns. In his dreams, he sees the stern face of his father, hears the disappointment in his voice: "How could you steal from me, your father? How could you secretly disobey me? Even now, after I ask for the truth, still you lie to me." Sundar knows this is not *dharma* – devotion. This is *adharma* – sin.

It is evil. The holy books speak of *karma* – the relentless cycle of sin and death by whose law every sinful act burdens the soul and carries painful consequences. The holy books warn that we will reap what we sow, in this life or the next. How can I escape this karma? How can I undo what I have done? What good is compassion for others in need if my own soul is burdened?

Sardar Sher Singh hears a quiet, frightened voice:

Father! Wake up, Father! Something terrible has happened. It was I, Father. I stole your money to buy a blanket for the widow. Forgive me, Father. I want to escape the karma; I am ready to accept punishment; I am ready to accept it as penance for this sin.

Now awake, Sardar Sher Singh sees the anguish in the boy's face and sees the hours of anguish behind it. He takes hold of the boy—not to punish him, but to take him up into his strong arms; not with anger, but with love. Gently he says: "I have always trusted you, my child, and now I have good proof that my trust was not misplaced. Sleep in peace now, for you have shown courage to choose what is right. In this way, you have turned the wrong to good. I, too, am sorry that I refused you money for the widow. I will not refuse you such a request again."

five holy men

Once in Haridwar I met a sadhu lying on a bed of nails. I went to him and asked, "To what end do you wound and torture yourself so?" He answered:

You are a sadhu yourself. Do you not know why I do this? It is my penance. I am destroying the flesh and its desires. I serve God in this way, but I still feel all too clearly the pain of my sins and the evil in my desires. Indeed, the pain of them is far worse than the pain of these nails. My goal is to kill all desire and so to find release from myself and oneness with God. I have been exercising this discipline for eighteen months, but I have not yet reached my goal. Indeed, it is not possible to find release in such a short time; it will take many years, even many lives, before I can hope for release.

I considered the life of this man. Must we torture ourselves through many lives in order to find true peace? If we do not reach our goal in this life, why should there be another chance in another life? Is it even possible in thousands on thousands of lives? Can such peace ever be found through our own efforts? Must it not be a gift from God? Surely we must seek the life of God, not the death of flesh.

I met another sadhu doing penance. His feet were tied with a rope and he was hanging upside down from the branch of a tree. When he had ended his exercise and was resting under the tree, I asked him, "Why do you do this? What is the purpose of such torture?" He answered:

People are greatly amazed to see me hanging head-down from a tree, but remember, the Creator sets every child head-down in the mother's womb. This is my method to serve God and do penance. In the eyes of the world it is folly, but in this exercise I remind myself and others that all of us are bound by sin and lead lives that are, in God's eyes, upside down. I seek to turn myself upside down again and again until in the end I stand upright in the sight of God.

It is true that the world is upside down and its ways are perverted. But can we ever hope to right ourselves through our own strength? Must we not turn instead to God, who alone can set right what is wrong and free us from evil thoughts and desires?

Later, I met yet another sadhu. In the hot summer, he would continually sit within the five fires—that is, with four fires around him and the burning sun overhead. In winter he would stand for hours in the icy water. Yet his whole expression was marked by sadness and despair. I learned that the man had been undergoing this exercise for five years. I approached him and asked: "What have you gained from this discipline? What have you learned?" He answered sadly, "I do not hope to gain or learn anything in this present life, and about the future I can say nothing."

The following day I went to see a sadhu who had taken an oath of silence. He was a genuine seeker after truth. He had not spoken for six years. I went to him and asked him questions: "Did God not give us tongues so that we can speak? Why do you not use yours to worship and praise the Creator instead of remaining silent?" Without any hint of pride or arrogance he answered me by writing on a slate:

> You are right, but my nature is so evil that I cannot hope for anything good to come out of my mouth. I have remained silent for six years, but my nature remains evil, so it is better that I remain silent until I receive some blessing or message that can help others.

Once in the Himalayas I learned of a Buddhist hermit, an old lama who lived in a cave in the mountains. He had closed off the entrance of the cave by building a stone wall—leaving only a small opening for air. He never left the cave and lived only from the tea and roasted barley that devout people brought and passed through the small hole. Because he had lived so long in utter darkness, he had become blind. He was determined to remain in the cave for the rest of his life. When I found this hermit, he was engaged in prayer and meditation, so I waited outside until he had finished. Then I asked if I might speak with him, and we were able to converse through the hole in the wall, although we could not see each other. First he asked me about my spiritual journey. Then I asked him, "What have you gained through your seclusion and meditation? Buddha taught nothing about a God to whom we can pray. To whom do you pray, then?" He answered:

> I pray to Buddha, but I do not hope to gain anything by praying and by living in seclusion. Quite the opposite, I seek release from all thought of gain. I seek nirvana, the elimination of all feeling and all desire—whether of pain or of peace. But still I live in spiritual darkness. I do not know what the end will be, but I am sure that whatever I now lack will be attained in another life.

I then responded:

> Surely your longings and feelings arise from the God who created you. They were surely created in order to be fulfilled, not crushed. The destruction of all desire cannot lead to

release, but only to suicide. Are not our desires inseparably intertwined with the continuation of life? Even the idea of eliminating desire is fruitless. The desire to eliminate all desire is still itself a desire. How can we find release and peace by replacing one desire with another? Surely we shall find peace not by eliminating desire, but by finding its fulfillment and satisfaction in the One who created it.

The hermit closed our conversation, saying, "We shall see what we shall see."

maya · *illusion*

The sunlight speckled with jungle shadows paints leopard spots on the hermit's yellow robe. The hermit, the old sadhu, the holy man sits cross-legged on a leopard skin, one with the skin, one with the leopard, one with the jungle.

At the feet of the sadhu sits Sundar, a boy fleeing *maya* — illusion — and hungry for certainty and knowledge — *jnana*. The boy is devout. He is a Sikh, a devout Sikh, a devout among the devout, a lion among the lions. But he is restless.

Sikh priests have taught him all they know, but he is not satisfied. He can recite the entire *Guru Granth Sahib,* the holy book of the Sikhs, but it does not quench his thirst. He can recite the *Upanishads,* the *Darsanas,* the *Bhagavad Gita* and the *Shastaras* of the Hindus; the *Qur'an* and the *Hadis* of Islam are known to him by heart. His mother fears God and sees in him a pilgrim; she sees in him the making of a sadhu. His father is worried. He asks Sundar: "Why do you torment yourself over religious questions? You will twist your brain and ruin your sight." The boy answers, "I must have *santi*. I must have peace."

In his quest, the boy has come to the old sadhu in the jungle:

Sadhu-ji, you say my hunger and my thirst are illusion, tricks of *maya*. Only *Brahma* is truth. *Brahma* is the divine source of all things, you say; *Brahma* is God. You say I will see that I am part of *Brahma*, and that once I do, my needs will cease to concern me. Forgive me, Sadhu-ji, and do not be angry with me, but how can this be? If I am *Brahma* or have even a part of it, how then can I be deceived by *maya*? How can illusion have power over me? For if illusion has power over truth, then truth is itself illusion. Is then illusion stronger than truth? Is illusion stronger than truth?

Sadhu-ji, you say I must wait. You say I will gain knowledge of spiritual things as I grow older. My thirst will be quenched. But can it be so? Is not food the answer to hunger? Is not water the answer to thirst? If a hungry boy asks for bread, can his father answer, "Go and play! When you are older, you will understand hunger and you will not need bread?" If you, Sadhu-ji, have found the understanding I seek, if you have found certainty and peace, please tell me how I can find it. If not, then tell me so, and I will continue my search. I cannot rest until I have found peace.

Something is wrong. Why do the *Shastaras* no longer come alive before my eyes? Why does our holy book now seem so distant? Why do I return from the peace of *yoga* meditation to find my heart still burdened with unrest?

An adolescent boy struggles to hold onto all that his mother taught him. It was so natural and so simple while she was alive, but since her death the spiritual exercises require so much effort. Faith has become clouded by doubt. The words of the old sadhu in the jungle sound like hollow promises, with boldness he questions the sadhu's teaching. The words of the *Vedas* and of *Guru Granth Sahib* no longer answer his seeking. Instead, question after question stumbles over one another, and all is confusion. The lives of those around him seem fraught with hypocrisy. Where is the fire and clarity of the early Sikh believers? And now Christian missionaries bring still another truth, but their arrival brings Sundar only further, deeper confusion.

This is not the truth of my mother, of our ancestors, of our culture. This is a foreign truth, one brought to us by outsiders who do not understand our ways. But why then does Father make me attend the Christian school? I would rather go to the state school at Sanewal. I am ready to walk the six miles through the desert. I am a Sikh. I will show them. I will show Father what I think of these colonialists and their western ways, their foreign faith...

When the elders come to him, Sardar Sher Singh cannot believe his ears. There must be some mistake. Quiet, respectful Sundar throwing stones at his teachers, disrupting classes, and mocking the missionaries — impossible! When Sardar Sher Singh goes to see for himself, he cannot believe his eyes. Yet there, in the courtyard of his own house, a group of teenage boys gather around his son, who first tears the Christian's holy book to shreds and then, in a frenzy of rage, hurls it into a fire. Never in the history of the village has anyone publicly burned a sacred book of any faith! And his own son! He rushes out in confusion and anger. He seizes Sundar:

Are you insane? Why would you do such a thing? Is this the respect for sacred things you learned at your mother's breast? Is this your thanks to those who teach you? You will not commit such blasphemy in my presence. As your father and head of this household, I command you to stop such insanity. There will be no more book burning here!

———

Peace is gone. No one is left. Mother is dead. Father is shamed. The sadhu in the jungle has no more to say. The holy writings are remote and foreign. Meditation offers escape, but no resolution, no realization. The ritual bath cleanses the body, but all is still dark within. The familiar words of the scriptures whirl in his mind. There is Guru Nanak: "I cannot live for a moment without you, O God. When I have you, I have everything. You are the treasure of my heart." And there is Guru Arjim: "We long only for you, O God. We thirst for you. We can only find rest and peace in you." That is the only hope. If there is a God, then let him reveal the way to peace. If there is no God, then there is no point in living.

The fifteen-year-old boy rises long before the sun. With solemn ritual he bathes and chants the ancient invocation as he has done every morning for as long as he can remember, just as his mother taught him. This morning will be the last time. He thinks of his mother and wonders if he will find her in the world beyond. At 5:00 a.m. the express train to Ludhiana will pass. It will pass over the tracks near the edge of Sardar Sher Singh's property. It will pass over the body of a desperate, confused young man. It will crush all doubts and drive all questions from his heart and head.

The prophecy of the Sikh priest nears fulfillment, for had he not said to Sardar Sher Singh: "Your son is not like the others. Either he will become a great man of God, or he will disgrace us all by going insane."

PARABLE

the saint

Many years ago there was a saint who after finishing his daily round of duties would go to a cave in a jungle to pray and meditate for hours. One day a philosopher happened to come across the cave. Finding the saint on his knees, he first stood there in amazement. Then he went up to the entrance of the cave and tapped, but the saint was so absorbed in contemplation that he did not respond. The philosopher waited at least half an hour and was on the point of leaving when the saint rose and called him in to sit down. Both remained silent for a few moments. Then the philosopher broke the silence.

Philosopher: Do you know that this cave is known as a den of robbers?

Saint: Yes, sir, I know it well. This cave is a meeting place for robbers but it is a shelter for me. When I am in the city in the midst of so many people, when I have done my work and want to pray and meditate, I find obstacles and impediments that disturb my worship and distract me so that neither I nor others receive any real benefit from my spiritual exercise. So I retire from the disturbances of city life to this quiet place and rest here in the presence of my God and worship him in the beauty of his holiness. Here I spend my time in prayer and offer intercessions on behalf of others. This spiritual exercise has done much good not only for me but for others as well.

Thieves often visit this place, but they never trouble me. One of them once said to me, "See, honorable saint, we are not blind and stupid. We rob those people who, though not called robbers, yet rob others as much as we do." I will not report them to the authorities, because I know a worldly government cannot reform them. It can only punish them and further harden their hearts. But I pray to God, who can change them and grant them new life. Some of them have already changed and become good citizens. So by the grace of God, my spiritual work is being carried on in this solitude in the same way as it is done among the multitudes.

Philosopher: You truly believe that you are helping others by sitting here silently and praying?

Saint: Some people equate watching and praying with laziness or carelessness. This is wrong. As a matter of fact, it means diving into the ocean of reality and finding pearls of divine truth that will enrich not only the diver, but others as well. As a diver holds his breath while he is diving, so a man of contemplation and prayer shuts himself in a chamber of silence, away from the distractions of the noisy world. Then he is able to pray with the Holy Spirit from above, without which it is impossible to lead a spiritual life.

My meaning is clear: God works in silence. No man has ever heard him speak or make any sound. To hear his voice, we must wait for him in silence. Then, without voice or words, he will speak to the soul in the secret room of the heart. As he himself is spirit, he addresses the soul in spiritual language, fills it with his presence, and finally revives and refreshes it forever.

Philosopher: Silence is important. I, too, know that if I do not concentrate silently, I cannot think. But I am not convinced about your silent God. What proof do you have for his existence?

Saint: Remember that though millions experience his presence, he exists above and beyond all human comprehension. He dwells only in the heart of those who have a childlike faith. As putting our hand near the flames and experiencing the warmth of the fire proves the existence of fire, so experiencing God in spirit is the only strong and solid proof of his existence. I know of a woman who, when she was twelve, was told by her teacher about God and his love. It was the first time she had ever heard of God, yet as her teacher spoke, she said, "Yes, I have known this already. I just did not know his name."

Philosopher: But why is it that you renounce the world? Do you hate the world and regard yourself as superior to others?

Saint: I do not hate the world, and I would never dare to regard myself superior to others – God forbid. I am only a weak and sinful man, but grace saves and helps me. Nor have I renounced the world. I renounce only its evil and everything in myself that hinders my spiritual life.

As long as we are in this world, it is impossible to renounce it. If we leave the city and go to live in the jungle, we will find that the jungle is also part of the world. It is ridiculous to think of renouncing the world. No one can renounce the world except through death. God put us on this earth to live and move and be. His holy will is that we may use the things of this world in the right way – to prepare ourselves for our true spiritual home.

Philosopher: If you are so weak and sinful, why do people call you a saint?

Saint: The Greek philosopher Socrates once said that in all his life, he had learned only one, single lesson—namely, that he knew nothing. Whenever people asked him what then the difference was between him and other folk, he replied that he differed from others only in one respect: he accepted that he knew nothing, while they obstinately clung to the belief that they knew something.

Let people think what they will, but I am no saint—they are mistaken. I only desire intimacy with God. In fellowship with him I experience a peace that is unknown to the worldly. I know that I am weak and sinful, but most people do not even know that they are sinners. Hence, they do not know the cure for their sin, and they die without ever finding the peace that I have found.

santi • *peace*

Though at the time I had considered myself a hero for burning the Gospel, my heart found no peace. Indeed, my unrest only increased, and I was miserable for the next two days. On the third day, when I could bear it no longer, I rose at 3:00 a.m. and prayed that if there was a God at all, he would reveal himself to me. Should I receive no answer by morning, I would place my head on the railroad tracks and seek the answer to my questions beyond the edge of this life.

I prayed and prayed, waiting for the time to take my last walk. At about 4:30 I saw something strange. There was a glow in the room. At first I thought there was a fire in the house, but looking through the door and windows, I could see no cause for the light. Then the thought came to me: perhaps this was an answer from God. So I returned to my accustomed place and prayed, looking into the strange light. Then I saw a figure in the light, strange but somehow familiar at once. It was neither Siva nor Krishna nor any of the other Hindu incarnations I had expected. Then I heard a voice speaking to me in Urdu: "Sundar, how long will you mock me? I have come to save you because you have prayed to find the way of truth. Why then don't you accept it?" It was then I saw the marks of blood on his hands and feet and knew that it was Yesu, the one proclaimed by the Christians. In amazement I fell at his feet. I was filled with deep sorrow and remorse for my insults and my irreverence, but also with a wonderful peace. This was the joy I had been seeking. This was heaven…Then the vision was gone, though my peace and joy remained.

When I arose I immediately went to wake my father and tell him what I had experienced – to tell him that I was now a follower of Yesu. He told me to go back to bed. "Why, only the day before yesterday you were burning the Christians' holy book. Now you say you are one of them. Go and sleep, my child. You are tired and confused. You will feel better in the morning."

Sardar Sher Singh tried to be understanding and patient, for he felt the boy was still distraught from the loss of his mother. So he discreetly avoided discussing Sundar's strange experience. Sundar in turn spent most of his time in solitude and meditation, seeking penance and wondering how to atone for his mockery of the One who had revealed himself to him. Deep within, he sensed that release would only come if he was prepared to serve Yesu as one serves a master – to publicly declare himself a follower of the very being he had publicly insulted.

No one could have foreseen the outcry that followed. Robbed of their ringleader, Sundar's peers turned on their Christian teachers (and on Sundar himself), hurling abuse, accusing them of forcibly converting the boy, despite Sundar's repeated assertions that the teachers knew nothing of what had happened. Feelings ran so high that the school had to be closed, and the missionaries escaped to Ludhiana.

At home Sardar Sher Singh tried everything he could to dissuade his son from his new-found faith. At first he exercised patience. Then he appealed to the boy's honor:

My dear son—light of my eyes, comfort of my heart— may you live long! As your father, I appeal to you to consider your family. Surely you do not want the family name to be blotted out. Surely this Christian religion does not teach disobedience to parents. I call on you to fulfill your duty and to marry. I have chosen your bride, as is our custom, and everything is prepared. As an engagement present I will give you a legacy of 150,000 rupees that will provide enough interest for you and your family to live comfortably for a lifetime. Your uncle will add to it a chest of gold.

I am not an unreasonable man, my child. But if you refuse me, I will know that you are determined to dishonor your family and I will have no alternative but to disown you. You wear the bracelet of the Sikh, you wear your hair uncut as is the sign of the Sikh, you bear the name of a Sikh. Have you forgotten the meaning of the name that our fathers adopted? Have you forgotten what it means to be a *Singh*?

No, Father; the name means "lion."

You know the meaning of your name, yet act like a jackal of the desert. Why? The time has come for you to make your choice.

Sundar Singh returned to his room and prayed. Then he cut off his hair.

———

The face of Sardar Sher Singh was dreadful to behold. Rage born of frustration, desperation and shame reddened his eyes. In the presence of the entire household, his heart heavy with grief, he led his son to the door as darkness was falling. Already death had taken his wife and one son; now he was to lose his beloved Sundar. But he saw no choice: the boy had made his decision. Now he spoke the fearful curse: "We reject you forever and cast you from among us. You shall be no more my son. We shall know you no more. For us, you are as one who was never born. I have spoken." The door closed behind him.

I will never forget the night I was driven out of my home. I slept outdoors under a tree, and the weather was cold. I had never experienced such a thing. I thought to myself: "Yesterday I lived in comfort. Now I am shivering, and I am hungry and thirsty. Yesterday I had everything I needed and more; today I have no shelter, no warm clothes, no food." Outwardly the night was difficult, but I possessed a wonderful joy and peace in my heart. I was following in the footsteps of my new master – of Yesu, who had nowhere to lay his head, but was despised and rejected. In the luxuries and comforts of home I had not found peace. But the presence of the Master changed my suffering into peace, and this peace has never left me.

PARABLE

the scholar

After his death, the soul of a German scholar entered into the world of spirits. From a distance he saw the indescribable glory of heaven and the unending joy of those who dwell there. He was overwhelmed by what he saw, but his intellect and his skepticism stood in his way and blocked his entrance to the realm of bliss. So he began to argue with himself:

> There can be no doubt that I see all this, but how can I be sure that it is real and not just a subconscious illusion? Let me apply the critical tests of science, logic, and philosophy; then we will see whether this apparent heaven really exists.

Now, the angels who dwelt in that place knew his thoughts and approached him, and one addressed him:

Your intellect has warped your entire being. If you want to see the world of the spirit, you must look with spiritual eyes. You must apply spiritual insight, not the rational exercise of logic. Your science deals with material reality. In this realm, however, you can only apply the wisdom that arises from love and reverence. It is a pity that you do not take to heart the words of the Master: "Unless you change completely and become like a little child, you shall not enter the heavenly realm."

Clearly you long to see spiritual truth. If you didn't—if your life and thoughts were only evil—you would not even see heaven from afar, as you do now. But until you tire of your folly and turn around, you will continue to wander the world, banging your philosophical head against reality. Only then will you gain true insight and be able to turn with joy to the light of God.

In a certain sense, all of space and time is spiritual. God's presence pervades everything. Thus all people live in the spiritual world. Each of us is a spiritual being clothed in a mortal body. But there is another level of reality where our spirits go and dwell after physical death. This can be understood as a kind of misty twilight between the glorious light of heavenly bliss and the frigidity and darkness of death. Already in this life we set the course that determines where we shall enter into the world beyond death. From there, we either turn joyfully toward the light, or rebelliously toward the darkness.

jnana • *knowledge*

Cast out of my father's house, I sought the advice of my former teachers at the missionary school. They provided for my material needs and arranged for me to go to the Christian Boys' Boarding School in Ludhiana. The people there received me very kindly and protected me in every way. But I was shocked to see the godlessness of some of the students, and of some of the local Christians. I had believed that Christians would be like living angels; in this I was sadly mistaken.

A newly captured tiger prowls restlessly, while a tiger that has been caged for a long time sprawls lazily, awaiting the next feeding. Sundar's thoughts fled the comfortable confines of the missionaries' kindness. Everything was available to him: a good education, a position in the colonial establishment. Everything would be given him if he accepted the cozy life of a good Christian boy. Yet on his sixteenth birthday, he disappeared into the jungle. He reappeared thirty-three days later in the saffron robe of a beggar-monk. No more a lion, he had become a tiger — a tiger that seeks the thorny tracks of the jungle. His pilgrimage had begun.

————

Two sadhus sit cross-legged and converse with one another. One is old, very old, the picture of wisdom with a long, gray beard and faded saffron robe. The other, Sundar, is young and strong—a slight hint of fuzz on his chin. The one is a tranquil hermit at Varanasi, where the brown water of the Ganges slowly flows in its ageless, unchanging course past masses of bathing pilgrims. The other is a wanderer seeking the source, seeking the mountains where the sacred river dances and leaps in rushing, unpredictable torrents.

Old sadhu: The ancient rules laid down for the way of the sadhu are wise. A man follows first the order of the student, gaining the knowledge and skills for a productive life. Next he takes on the order of father, caring for family and property to exercise responsibility. Then, when his duties of the second order are fulfilled, he retires from the affairs of family and household, adopting the ascetic order of the sadhu and renouncing the comfort and pleasures of this world. In this way, he can offer penance for the failings of this life and all the lives that have gone before; he can restore his karma.

Young sadhu: I am not opposed to the ancient customs, but my motive in becoming a sadhu is different from yours. I have not become a sadhu because I think that there is any merit or salvation to be gained by it. I long only to serve God the Master with all my heart and soul and mind and strength and to love my fellow men and women even as I love myself. If we allow this principle to guide our lives, then selfishness will flee from our hearts and we shall be like children of God. We will find in every man and woman our own brother and sister. This is the only salvation; this is the only release from karma, from the cycle of sin and death. So I lay aside all worldly encumbrances and lead the life of a sadhu not to gain release from karma, but in thankfulness to God, who has already released me.

Let one of your disciples come with two mangoes, one ripe and juicy, the other skin and stone with all the juice sucked out. What would you say if he gave you the withered fruit and sat down to enjoy the delicious fruit himself?

Old sadhu: Such behavior would be inexcusable. It would be an insult and the height of disrespect.

Young sadhu: Well, if in the days of our youth we waste ourselves in our own pleasures and then, in the weakness of old age, offer in service to God only the bones and skin of our former strength, have we not also acted selfishly and treated God with disrespect?

Where the wild, rushing Ganges leaves the Himalayas near Rishikesh, there is the thick, wild jungle of Kajliban, a place of complete seclusion that few pilgrims penetrate. Two bamboo cutters discovered there the collapsed form of a sadhu in a clearing, too weak to speak or move. They took him to a village where he was nursed back to health with milk and broth and sago.

After several years of service, I felt led to go into the forest, where I would be free from interruption. I could fast for forty days even as the Master had done, and I could seek blessing on my past work and strength for my future work. Soon I was so dehydrated and enervated that I could not even move into the shade. But my spiritual awareness grew correspondingly sharper. Through this I discovered that the soul does not fade and die with the body, but goes on living, and I sensed the presence of God and the fullness of the Spirit, a reality that cannot be expressed in words. I also had a vision of the Master, though this time with spiritual – not physical – eyes.

Throughout the fast, I felt a remarkable enrichment of the peace and bliss that I had known in varying degrees since my first vision of the Master. Indeed, so great was this sense of peace that I was not at all tempted to break the fast. The experience has had a lasting effect on me. Before it, I was frequently assailed by temptations. Especially when I was tired, I often grew annoyed when people came to talk to me and ask me questions. I still grow irritated at times, but not as often as I used to. Moreover, I used to toy at times with the thought of giving up the self-denial required of a sadhu – of getting married and living in comfort and ease. Now, however, I see clearly that my calling is different, and that the gift of ecstasy God has given me is far better than any home, and far greater than any hardship I might endure.

––––––

"He's back! The Sadhu has returned!" The news ran like wildfire through the dingiest alleys of Kotgahr. No adult took notice; few even heard the excited cries above the din of the marketplace. But the children – the dirty toddler with the bloated stomach; the girl with the maimed foot; the boy with the scarred face; the scrawny offspring of the lepers, shunned even by the Untouchables – they heard the cries. Sundar Singh was back – and he was there again for them. And so they hurried – running, scuffling and limping – to his cave. It would be impossible to imagine a happier band of children.

Meanwhile, many miles away, among the students of the Christian Boys' Boarding School, Sundar Singh was changing the lives of other children too. C. F. Andrews, a close friend of the Sadhu, remembers:

Whenever Sundar Singh was in town, he spent most of his spare time visiting the boys in the school. They sat up with him into the long hours of the night and became intensely eager to go to Kotgahr and live with him there, so that they might catch something of his brave spirit.

The changes that resulted were marvelous to witness. One of the students, a cricketer and athlete, gave up assured prospects in government service for a life of Christian service. Another made up his mind to enter the ministry of the Church for a life of sacrifice and devotion. When one of the school sweepers, an Untouchable, fell ill, one of the boys who had come most under the influence of the Sadhu, went into the sweepers' quarters, stayed with him and nursed him through his illness. Such a thing had never happened in the history of the school.

One of the senior students returned late one evening, carrying on his back a man from the hills who was in the last stage of a terrible infectious disease. The boy had found him in an unfrequented place at the edge of the jungle, where he had been lying neglected, possibly for some days. Without a thought he loaded the man on his back and carried him for nearly two miles along a mountain track. Even the physical feat was remarkable; but the moral stamina that made him ready to risk a dangerous disease while others had passed by was more noteworthy still. Only because he was living with the Sadhu, did the inspiration come to this young man with such compelling force as to make him act in this manner. Still further, the humility and reticence with which this brave deed was done were themselves a reflection of the Sadhu's spirit.

What, it may be asked, was the attraction that made such a wonderful change? Nothing that was merely second-rate could possibly have effected it. No mode of living, half in comfort, half in self-denial, could have worked such a miracle. Indeed, those of us who did our work surrounded by too much outward comfort did not impress the young people. We did not think it possible for us to change our style of living, though we often talked the matter over. But Sundar Singh's life could stand the test. It was reckless in its self-spending. He had counted the cost. The Cross was not preached only, but lived – and that made all the difference.

II. conversations

PARABLE

the pilgrim

There is a deep and natural craving in the human heart that can be satisfied nowhere except in God. Our being in this world is a test, a preparation for the deepest state of spiritual communion. But most of us, suppressing our deepest longings and disdaining God, seek satisfaction from this world. Such a path can only lead to despair.

The story is told of a man who made it his goal in life to find peace and to satisfy all his desires. He thought that if he wandered the world, he would be sure to find a place where he could live a life of peace and rest without having to work or worry or suffer pain. Having made careful preparations, he set out on his journey. For months he wandered from place to place but could not find what he was seeking. One day he saw an old man sitting by the edge of a new grave. The traveler came closer and asked the old man whose grave it was. The man told him a remarkable story:

Two woodcutters from my village went out into the nearby jungle to cut wood. By chance, I was also walking that way. I saw them and greeted them from a distance. They were seated near a bush in conversation and did not notice me. So I approached them, and as I came closer, one of them saw me and quickly covered something with a cloth. I asked him what was under the cloth. At first, the men tried to evade my question and keep their secret hidden. So I asked again. Finally, they told me their story, saying that I was to be the judge of what had happened, and I was to give them my advice.

One of the men told me that as they were walking through the forest, they noticed something glittering under the bush. Coming closer, they found two gold ingots. When I arrived, they were debating what to do with this treasure. I told them that these bars were death traps in the guise of gold and they should be left under the bush and forgotten. I explained to them that I had heard about a banker in a nearby town who had been killed by burglars in his house. If the thieves were somewhere about and discovered the woodcutters with their treasure, they would not hesitate to kill them. Moreover, if the woodcutters kept the gold and were discovered, they would surely be accused of the theft and the banker's murder. They nodded in agreement and said they would do as I suggested. Then I went on my way.

However, they continued to argue over the gold, ignoring my advice. The first woodcutter demanded two-thirds share, because according to him, it was he who had discovered the gold; the other insisted that they should divide it equally. Finally, the first agreed. To celebrate, one of them went into the village to buy something to eat.

Once separated, however, both men burned with such greed that each plotted to kill the other. When the woodcutter who had gone into the village returned, the one who had remained to watch over the gold attacked him and killed him. But the murderer did not live to enjoy the gold, because—not knowing that his companion had poisoned the food he had bought—he ate of it and fell dead. Now both of them lie in this grave.

Looking over to another grave with a marble headstone, the traveler asked the old man, "Whose grave is that there?" The old man shook his head thoughtfully and said:

That man was exceedingly rich. But now he is dead, and what use is his fancy monument? And look over there. Do you see that mound? That was a man who was proud and cruel, using violence and smooth words to take over a kingdom. Once he was in power, he demanded that all the citizens should satisfy his desires and worship him as a god. Then he was stricken with a fatal disease, and worms fed on him till he died. A few days after his burial, wild animals dug his body from the grave and feasted on it, scattering his bones over the graveyard. The head that had borne a crown was now a bare skull on the ground.

As the traveler was pondering the meaning of what was being said, the old man continued:

These stories illustrate human depravity, but there is also a solution. There is a stream of love in this world that gives health, joy, and peace. Those who live in this current of love (which is God) always try to do good to others and never return evil for evil.

There was once a widow who, after mourning the death of her husband, had a dispute with her sister over the distribution of the property. Finally, the widow's sister became so angry that she took the widow's son and abandoned him in a basket in the river. A fisherman who found the child took him home and brought him up as his own son. The boy grew into manhood. One day, while selling fish in the marketplace, he unwittingly met his mother. Though she did not recognize the young man as her son, she felt pity for him, and invited him and the old fisherman to come and live with her.

Not long afterwards the widow noticed among the fisherman's possessions a basket she recognized as her own. She also noticed, on the boy's elbow, a familiar scar that identified him as her son.

Confronting her sister later, the widow, however, wrung a confession from her. Her anger knew no bounds. Thankfully, she was kept from taking revenge, for the boy held his mother back and prevented her from retaliating. Serving both his mother and his aunt for the rest of his days, he showed, by his acts of kindness and mercy, how evil is overcome only with good.

The traveler thanked the old man for his stories and set off down the road. On the way he met an athlete and a leper talking together. "How did you get leprosy?" the athlete asked. "I have been told that it is because I lived in evil and immorality," the leper replied. "You have kept yourself in good health and your body is strong. But in the end, your body and mine shall be the same—dust in the earth."

The traveler continued on his way, thinking. He saw now that his longing for a life of comfort and ease was mere selfishness, and that only a life lived for others and for God would bring him true freedom. To live selfishly, he saw, is to flap like a bird that has escaped its cage, only to realize it is still tethered. The harder it struggles, the more entangled it becomes.

It has been well observed that though nations may differ from nations, communities from communities, and people from people, human nature is the same everywhere. As there is but one sun that warms and gives light to the earth, there is but one God who teaches us to love one another and care for each other.

It is not just the widows, orphans, the poor, and the needy that are unhappy. Kings in their kingdoms, the wealthy in the midst of their luxury, and the learned with their wisdom are also restless and unfulfilled. As with Noah's dove, which found no place to rest in the world, so it is with us. As strangers and pilgrims on the earth, we can find no rest without the Master who said, "Come to me, all who labor and are heavy laden, and I will give you rest."

darshana • *the divine presence*

Seeker: Sadhu-ji, I am searching for inner peace, but the many religions and philosophies I have studied fill me only with doubts and questions. I am no longer even sure if God exists. Can you help me find spiritual truth?

Sadhu: Only the fool says in his heart, "There is no God." Such a thought says nothing about the existence or nonexistence of God, but only about the skeptic's own spiritual blindness and inability to recognize God. Indeed, atheists deny the existence of God altogether, but they cannot prove their claim that God does not exist. Even if we assume for the sake of argument that they are correct, we would only further the cause of ignorance, not the cause of truth, because what could be a greater waste of time than to try and prove the nonexistence of something that doesn't even exist? Time would be better spent on more worthwhile pursuits. Yet if God does exist, as all spiritually enlightened souls know, then it would be still greater foolishness to try and prove God's nonexistence. Though many argue that the belief in God is a harmful superstition that must be eliminated for the sake of human progress, the opposite is the case. Uncounted spiritual blessings have enriched the lives of those who believe.

Unlike atheists, agnostics believe neither in the existence nor in the nonexistence of God. They claim that we cannot know whether God exists. But again this is a mistake. We have an innate longing in our hearts to know God, and every race in every age has shown in some form or another its deep craving for God. Is God simply a human invention, as an ancient philosopher once said? He argued the following: "In the primeval age of disorder and violence, as always, laws could punish crimes committed in the open day, but they could not touch the secret crimes hidden in the gloomy depths of conscience. So the best way to make people lead moral lives was to make them afraid by inventing gods who could see and hear all things, not only all human actions, but also the inmost thoughts and intentions of the human heart." Yet, even this argument actually acknowledges that the human soul is incomplete and unfulfilled without God.

Some claim that God is unknowable, but this is utter nonsense. Such an assertion can only be made on the basis of some kind of limited knowledge of God. If

God is completely beyond our knowing, how can we know that he is unknowable?

Seeker: Can no one prove to me whether God exists, so that I can know the truth?

Sadhu: God has no need or desire for anyone to prove his existence. Our arguments are feeble, our minds limited. God could have provided proofs convincing enough, way beyond anything we could imagine. God desires rather that we should enjoy his life-giving presence and so bear witness to something far more sublime and convincing than anything the rational mind can produce.

Our spirits live and grow in our human bodies much like the chick develops inside the egg. If it were possible for the chick to be told that a great world waits beyond its shell, that this world is filled with fruits and flowers, rivers and great mountains, and that its own mother is also there waiting for it to be set free and to experience this splendor, the chick could still neither comprehend nor believe it. Even if one explained that its feathers and wings and eyes were developing so that it could fly and see, still it would not be able to believe it, nor would any proof be possible, until it broke through its shell.

In the same way, there are many people who cannot comprehend the spiritual life or the existence of God because they cannot see beyond the confines of their bodily sense. Their thoughts – like delicate wings – cannot yet carry them beyond the narrow confines of logic. Their weak eyes cannot yet make out those eternal treasures that God has prepared for his children. The only condition necessary for us to break out of our material limitations and attain spiritual life is that we accept the life-giving warmth of God's spirit, just as the chick receives its mother's warmth. Without that warmth, we will not take on the nature of the Spirit and we may die without ever hatching out of this material body.

We have been endowed with spiritual senses so that we can feel and enjoy God's presence. But the influence of irreverence and sin deadens these senses till we are no longer able to see beyond ourselves, nor beyond the material world. As long as we follow this path, we cannot believe that God exists, and so we starve ourselves until in the end we have committed spiritual suicide. Our end is total enslavement to the material world.

Seeker: If we cannot prove that God exists, then how can we ever know God or any spiritual truth?

Sadhu: God is the author of creation and provides all that is necessary for our wellbeing. If it were helpful or necessary for us to know God perfectly already now, then God would have provided the means to meet that need. Quite the contrary, it is important for our own spiritual growth that we persevere in trying to know more of God. True and satisfying knowledge of anything is always the fruit of mental exertion and the exercise of our own consciousness.

God is infinite while we are finite. We can never fully comprehend the infinite, but we do have within us a spiritual sense that allows us to recognize and enjoy God's presence. The ocean is vast beyond our imagining, and it would never be possible for a person to fathom it or take in all its great treasures. But with the tip of our tongues we can recognize at once that the ocean is salty. We have not understood even a fraction of all there is to know about the ocean, but with our sense of taste we can experience its essence.

In the end, how can we expect to have full knowledge of the creator, when even our knowledge of created things is limited? We know a little about the physical characteristics of the created world, but we know next to nothing about the unseen spiritual world. Indeed, we know next to nothing about our own spiritual lives. If we had complete knowledge of our own spiritual nature, then perhaps we would be capable of knowing the nature of God, for we were created in his image.

From the moment of birth, every child loves its mother dearly in its own way, but the child cannot know and love the mother as the mother loves the child. With age, the child grows to know the mother better and to enjoy her company in new, fulfilling ways. Our knowledge and age would have to be infinite if we were to truly comprehend God who is infinite. But at every age and level of knowledge we can appreciate and enjoy some aspect of God's presence. Why do we need to know more than this? As we grow spiritually, we will come to know more and more of God, but there is no need to be impatient. Eternity stretches before us.

One day I saw a flower and began to contemplate its fragrance and beauty. As I thought more deeply, I recognized the creator of such wonders – not with my mortal eyes but with my spiritual eyes. This filled my heart with joy, but my joy was still greater when I recognized that same creator at work within my own soul. How wonderful is God, separate from creation and yet ever filling it with his glorious presence.

Seeker: Since we know so little about God's nature, how is it even possible to recognize his divine presence?

Sadhu: Many people experience the Master's presence without actually seeing him. When we apply medicine drops to our eyes, we experience the healing effect, but we cannot see the drops. In the same way, we recognize the presence of the Master and his work of cleansing our inner eyes and aiding our spiritual sight even though we cannot see him.

Those who turn to the Master with open hearts will feel his power and experience peace. It is like something sweet on the tongue. Both our sense of taste and the sweetness of the sugar are invisible to the eye. Similarly, the Master sustains us with unseen nourishment—wisdom that the five senses cannot grasp.

God is revealed in the book of nature for God is its author. Yet we only comprehend this book if we have the necessary spiritual insight. Without reverence and perception we go astray. We cannot judge the truthfulness of any book merely by reading it. Agnostics and skeptics, for example, find only defects instead of perfection. Skeptics ask, "If there is an almighty creator, why then are there hurricanes, earthquakes, pain, suffering, death, etc.?" This is like criticizing an unfinished building or incomplete painting. When we see them fully finished, we are embarrassed at our own folly and praise the skill of the artist. God did not shape the world into its present form in a single day, nor will it be perfected in a single day. The whole creation moves toward completion, and if we see it with the eyes of God moving toward the perfect world without fault or blemish, then we can only bow humbly before our creator and exclaim, "It is very good."

Seeker: From what you say, Sadhu, it seems to require patience and great effort to recognize God's presence. What do we actually gain by seeking God?

Sadhu: A mother once left her child for a time playing in the garden. When her little son noticed she was not there, he searched the whole garden over. He looked everywhere but could not find her. Finally he cried and called out, but still she did not appear. The gardener saw him crying and tried to calm him, saying: "Do not cry! Look at these beautiful flowers and delicious mangoes. Shall I pick some for you?" But the child answered: "No! No! My mother has better food than these mangoes and her love is far sweeter than all these flowers. I want my mother." When his mother heard these words, she rushed out, embraced him, and smothered him with kisses. At that moment, the garden became a paradise. This world is like a great garden full of wonderful and beautiful flowers, but we cannot find true joy in it until we meet God.

Seeker: So how do I find the path to spiritual truth and to knowledge of God?

Sadhu: God never discourages a seeker by judging his or her beliefs to be wrong. Rather, God allows each person to recognize spiritual error or truth by degrees. The story is told of a poor grass cutter who found a beautiful stone in the jungle. He had often heard of people finding valuable diamonds and thought this must be one. He took it to a jeweler and showed it to him with delight. Being a kind and sympathetic man, the jeweler knew that if he bluntly told the grass cutter that his stone was worthless glass, the man would either refuse to believe it or else fall into a state of depression. So instead, the jeweler offered the grass cutter some work in his shop so that he might become better acquainted with precious stones and their value.

Meanwhile, the man kept his stone safely locked away in a strongbox. Several weeks later, the jeweler encouraged the man to bring out his own stone and examine it. As soon as he took it out of the chest and looked at it more closely, he immediately saw that it was worthless. His disappointment was great, but he went to the jeweler and said: "I thank you that you did not destroy my hope but aided me instead to see my mistake on my own. If you will have me, I will stay with you and faithfully serve you, as you are a good and kind master." In the same way, God leads back to truth those who have wandered into error. When they recognize the truth for themselves, they gladly and joyfully give themselves in obedient service.

Some say that desire is the root cause of all pain and sorrow. According to this philosophy, salvation consists in eliminating all desire, including any desire for eternal bliss or communion with God. But when someone is thirsty, do we tell him to kill his thirst instead of giving him water to drink? To drive out thirst without quenching it with life-sustaining water is to drive out life itself. The result is death, not salvation. Thirst is an expression of our need for water and a sign of hope that somewhere there is water that can satisfy our thirst. Similarly, the deep longing in our soul is a clear sign of hope that spiritual peace exists. Something can satisfy our thirsty souls. When the soul finds God, the author of that spiritual thirst, it receives far greater satisfaction than any thirsty man who receives water. When the soul's desire is satisfied, we have found heaven.

The water of a river that has its source in one country may flow through many different countries before it reaches the sea. It passes within the domain of many chiefs, rajahs, and princes. Yet no country has the right to stop it and keep it within its territory. It is the common property of all, and wherever it goes, it quenches the thirst of all. In the same way, the stream of life comes forth from the ocean of God's love, streaming to earth again as rain and then flowing as a river through the channels of the prophets and holy ones to irrigate the world. In this way, it quenches thirsty souls, enriching and restoring the lives of people and nations everywhere. Whoever desires it can freely take of this gift of life.

Seeker: If this life is freely given, then does God expect nothing from us? Don't we owe him some kind of worship?

Sadhu: People are foolish to believe that they confer some favor on God by their worship. Those who approach worship with such an attitude know nothing of the true nature of God. If we love God with all our heart, mind, soul, and strength, and if we love our neighbor as ourselves, then we will experience God's presence. This is worship. Eternal life will spring forth in our hearts; the fire of love will melt and forge us anew into the image of our creator.

The Master has said, "Love your neighbor as yourself." It is not hard to live for a few days in peace with someone — even one who is unfriendly. But if someone lives near us and annoys us day in and day out, then it becomes a difficult task even to endure — much less to love — that person. Yet if we can win through this great struggle, then we will find it all the easier to love others.

God is love, and the ability to love is inborn in every living creature, most especially in human beings. It is only right therefore that the Lover who has given us life and love itself should also receive love from us. God's love is creative and selfless, giving itself for the joy and benefit of creation. If we do not love God with all our heart and soul and mind and strength and if we do not love others freely and selflessly, then the love within us loses its divine character and turns to selfishness. Love then becomes a curse. Ironically, those who are selfish end up destroying themselves.

avatara • *incarnation*

Seeker: Sadhu-ji, I see that you live in deep inner peace, and I, too, long to find this peace. Can we imperfect mortals ever hope to experience true oneness with God?

Sadhu: We all have a natural, inborn desire to see God. But God is infinite and incomprehensible. No one can see God without being of the same infinite nature as God. We are finite, and so we cannot see God. But God is love. He is also the source of our craving to know and love him. Out of this love God took on a form that is comprehensible to us mortal beings. Through this act of love we can now share in the joy of the angels by seeing and knowing God directly. This is why the Master said: "Whoever has seen me has seen the Father."

God knows well the inner state of every human being and reveals himself to each heart in accordance with its needs. There is no better way for a person to enter true spiritual life than by encountering God directly. God became man and dwelt among us so that we might not fear him as something terrible and foreign, but instead see that God is love.

Seeker: I can understand that the infinite God is incomprehensible to us mortals. I can also understand that the power, or spirit of God, is at work around us. But how can this God be a man as well? This seems impossible.

Sadhu: The Almighty God and God Incarnate and God the Spirit are one. In the sun, there is heat and light and they are all one. But the heat is not the light and the light is not the heat. So it is with God. The Master and the Spirit both proceed from the Father to bring light and heat to the world. God the Spirit is fire that burns away all evil, making our hearts pure and holy. The Master is the true light that drives out all darkness and leads us to bliss along the path of truth. Yet all three are one, just as the sun is one.

Seeker: Tell me more about this Master of yours. Did he write down instructions for us to follow like other religious teachers?

Sadhu: The Master never wrote anything down, nor did he ask his followers to record his teachings. His words are spirit and life. Spirit can only infuse spirit. Life can only infuse life. The Master's teaching cannot be contained on the pages of a book. Other great teachers left behind books to replace the living voice, to guide and help their bereft followers. But the Master did not do this, because he has not left us. He is always with us, and his living voice guides and counsels us. His followers recorded his teachings after his ascension as a help to those who cannot yet perceive his living presence. In the end, however, when people ask me, "What made you a follower of the Master?" I can only answer: the Master.

Seeker: But don't your scriptures reveal the truth about God?

Sadhu: They reveal much to us about the life and teachings of the Master and about the nature of God's love. God the Spirit is the true author of the Bible, but this does not mean that every word, taken on its own, is holy or inspired. It is not the words in themselves, but rather the meaning that is inspired. The language used by those who wrote the books of the Bible was the language of everyday, not the language of spirit. Only when we make direct contact with the author, that is, with God the Spirit, can the meaning become clear. Just as many do not understand the Master, so too, they can not understand his words.

Seeker: I want to believe the truth of what you say, for I see its fruits in the peace you experience, but it is difficult for me to understand or accept.

Sadhu: God has created us with spiritual faculties and powers, but these must be used or else they will decay and be lost. Faith must be fixed on the living God or else irreverence and sin will rule; they will lead to doubt and ultimately destroy all faith.

Sometimes people say that they are ready to believe in God if only this or that doubt is removed or satisfied. Can one go to a doctor and ask that the pain of a broken arm be removed before the bone is set? This would be ridiculous because the pain is the result of the break. Once the limb has been set, the pain will pass away by itself. Doubts are spiritual pains that arise from our sin. Irreverence has broken our spiritual oneness with God. We must first restore spiritual union with God; then doubts with regard to the existence of God or the divinity of the Master will disappear on their own. Only then will the pain fade. Only then will we experience the wonderful spiritual peace that the world can neither give nor take away. The Master reveals God to us so that the union between God and us sinful humans might be restored. He has opened the way for us to enter his heavenly realm. Whoever sincerely seeks truth with an open heart will find it revealed in the Master.

We do not need knowledge of Hebrew or Greek, but we do need to be united with the Spirit. This Spirit guided the prophets and followers who recorded his words, and this spirit alone can reveal their true meaning to us. The language of the Master is spiritual, and we can only understand its meaning if we are awake in spirit. We do not need to know or understand anything about theological questions or criticisms. Indeed, a child can most readily grasp the Master's teaching, for the child is still united with the spiritual world from which it came. But those who possess wisdom that is only of this world can never understand, for the Master's spirit is not in them.

Seeker: If sin and irreverence have broken our relationship with God, then can't we restore it simply by leading a righteous life?

Sadhu: A cobra remains a cobra, no matter how many times it sheds its skin. There was once a village girl who daily dusted the cobwebs from her house. Once as she was doing this, she also prayed, "O God, as I am cleaning this room, please also cleanse my heart." Then she heard a voice saying: "Daughter, you will have to cleanse the room again and again as long as the spiders remain. It is better that you drive the spiders from your house." But she was not able to drive them out because they were hidden from her and too clever to be caught. Likewise, we see the signs of sin in our lives and struggle against them, but only God can remove the roots of sin from our souls.

Some moral teachers and many religious leaders say, "Do good works and you will become good people." It is absurd to suggest that a bitter tree will become sweet by constantly bringing forth fruit. A bitter tree can only become sweet by being grafted onto a sweet tree. The life and qualities of the sweet tree can then flow with its sap into the bitter tree, driving out all its inherent bitterness. In this way the tree becomes a new creation, capable of bearing sweet fruit.

We may well have the longing to do what is right, but everything we do is corrupted, tainted by our own selfishness and sin. Only if we recognize our sinfulness, as well as our inability to do what is right, and turn to the Master who grafts us onto himself, do we become new creations. Only then are we capable of doing good works. So I say, "First become good, and then you can perform good deeds."

Once a young man fell over a cliff. By the time he was rescued he had lost so much blood that he was almost dead. His father rushed him to a doctor, but the doctor said: "He will certainly die, unless someone can be found who is willing to provide enough blood for a massive transfusion." Now the father's heart overflowed with such love for his son that he offered his own blood, though he knew it would cost him his own life. So by the sacrificial love of his father, the young man was given new life. We, too, have fallen headlong from the mountain of righteousness and lie broken and wounded by sin, with our life fast ebbing away. But if we turn to the Master, he freely gives us his spiritual blood so that we might be saved from death and regain life. Indeed, he came to us for this very purpose.

PARABLE

the lovers

God is love. In love, God created human

beings in his own image, to love their creator with heart and
soul, to rejoice in his endless love and to love one another. But
because of sin, we love created things. We have forgotten God's
original love, the only genuine love. But sometimes it happens
that our distorted human love leads us back to divine love.

It is told that there was once a young man who belonged
to a respectable family and who, after finishing his studies
and other duties, used to go out for a walk in the jungle each
evening. His parents loved him dearly because of his good
character, amiable disposition, orderly habits, and obedience.
He was the pride of the family. One day he went farther than

usual into the jungle. In fear that darkness might overtake him, he frantically tried to find his way. Just as he reached the road, a wild beast attacked and wounded him. With his last strength, he drove off the beast, cried out for help and then collapsed from shock and exhaustion.

Some distance away a beautiful girl was gathering firewood. When this horrible cry reached her ears, she was at first frightened, but she took courage and went to see who had cried out so desperately. She found the handsome young man lying half-conscious with no one nearby to help him. He was badly wounded and bleeding heavily. She pitied him and led him by the hand to the nearby river. She washed his wounds, and tearing her own dress, she bandaged them. Then she struggled to help him reach his own village.

Finally, they reached the house of the young man. His parents and relatives were shocked to see him in such a frightful state. They were also distressed to see him in the company of the girl who was obviously poor and, in their eyes, quite beneath his social position. When the young man and the girl told their story, the lad's parents thanked the girl for her help and invited her to stay with them for the night, but they were actually eager to see her on her way. Early in the morning, the young man sent for her to express his deep gratitude. As soon as he saw her bright and beautiful face glowing in the morning light he was overwhelmed by her innocence, tenderness, and beauty. He fell in love with her in that instant and made up his mind to marry her at all costs. But the girl belonged to a very poor and low caste, and he knew this would be a great obstacle to overcome.

After hearing the young man's words of gratitude, the girl headed home. On her way through the jungle, she picked up the bundle of firewood she had left behind the day before and reached her village about midday. About the same time, her parents and relatives returned exhausted and desperate from their fruitless search through the night. Needless to say, they were greatly astonished to find the girl at home. The girl told the whole story in all simplicity and honesty, but nobody believed her. Her elder brother doubted her character and chastity and thought that she had run away and disgraced the name of the whole family. Her father beat the innocent girl black and blue and forbade her to step out of the house.

In time, the young man heard about how she had been treated, and so he decided to visit her. He went to her village and told her parents the whole story, but they did not believe him either, for there was no witness to verify it. The girl, who was listening eagerly to the young man, remained silent. The sweetness of his words and the brightness of his face mesmerized her. When he had left, she told her parents, "If you doubt my chastity, then please let me marry this young man." But her parents were very angry and refused. On his return home, the young man told his parents that he loved the girl who had rescued him and wanted to marry her. They became red with rage, punished him severely, and said: "Can't you find any better girl than this one of low and poor caste? Why do you want to disgrace our respectable family?"

Eventually, the young man slipped away unobserved, and went to the village of his beloved. By chance, she was alone in the house that day. So they talked together freely and frankly. They were able to meet a number of times in this way and their love grew ever deeper. But their parents were angry and bitterly spoke against their children's wishes. It thus became increasingly difficult for them to see each other. So they arranged to meet late at night when others were asleep. Sometimes the young man waited outside the girl's village and sometimes the girl waited near her lover's room.

One night there was an accident. The girl fell down a steep bank behind the boy's house and injured her leg. The young man heard the noise and came out at once. He discovered that her leg was broken, took her to the hospital, and made all the necessary arrangements for her care. He went daily to see her. After some days she felt much better. When her parents finally found out where she was, they took her away from the hospital and hid her with some relatives in a distant village.

The next day the young man went to the hospital as usual, but was confused when he did not find her there. The doctor in charge of the ward told him that she had recovered and that her parents had taken her home. The young man ran at once to her village, but she was not there. He feared that she had deceived him and had run away with some other man. Nevertheless, he missed her terribly and worried constantly. He could not find any clue where she might be. The girl also worried and wept bitterly day and night. Days passed but she heard nothing from her lover, so she also thought that perhaps he had forgotten her and had fallen in love with some other girl. In addition, her parents were arranging for her to marry another man.

One day, when her family was asleep, the girl slipped out and ran to her lover's house. Calling at his window, she discovered that he was not there. She wept bitterly, saying: "Alas! My parents and relatives are now my enemies. The man to whom I gave my heart has also left me. I cannot live another day in this world that is now hell to me." Thinking thus, she turned her steps toward the very river where she had once washed her lover's wounds. There, she jumped into the water, intending to end her life.

Nearby, her lover sat behind a large rock, absorbed in his thoughts and entirely unaware of the presence of his beloved. Hearing the sound of someone falling in the water, he leapt in and rescued the girl. It was all like a dream. He held the unconscious form of his beloved on his lap. After a few minutes, she revived and looked up into the dear face of her lover. All the bitterness of her life vanished in the twinkling of an eye. They embraced and kissed each other. At first, they were so overcome by joy that neither could speak. For half an hour they embraced each other with the deepest affection. Then they began to converse:

Lover: My beloved, how did you fall into the water? If I had not been here, your life would have ended.

Beloved: My darling, I waited so long for you and you didn't come. Then I went to your house to see you. When I did not find you there, I came here in despair and jumped into the river. There was no other way to put out the fire of separation and end the bitterness of my life. Without you my life appeared to me like hell. But tell me, why did you come here?

Lover: I came here with a similar determination. When you disappeared from the hospital I wandered about, searching long for you, but you were nowhere to be found. In my despair, I became weary of my life and wanted to die rather than face another day without you. I was on the point of committing suicide when I heard you leap into the water. Had you delayed even a few minutes, we both would have lost our lives in the same river, this river where you once washed my wounds. What a marvelous thing! Here you once saved my life and now it is I who have saved yours. Today we have both received a new life. Let us therefore lead it in a new way.

Surely, it was not we ourselves, but God who has given us this new life and united us again. As a sign of our gratitude we should now worship him and walk according to his will, because he alone is the source of life. Let us go to the man of prayer who once came to me and comforted me when I was lonely and heartbroken. His words of sympathy applied a wonderful and soothing balm to my aching wounds. It was he who told me that without the love of the Creator, the love of the creature is incomplete and can only breed restlessness and grief. I learned that God is always with us and that real happiness is found only in his presence. So, let us go to that man of prayer and he will marry us.

Beloved: My only longing is to follow you wherever you go and to serve you with all my heart and soul. Yes, I am ready to give my life to God and to you. A Hindu widow willingly gives herself to be burnt alive with the dead body of her husband. Would it not be shameful, if I am not ready to give my life in service to the living God and to his servant, my dear husband? But what will become of us? I am of a very poor and low caste. Our parents are already very angry and will never accept our marriage.

Lover: My beloved, had I taken pride in caste or social standing, I would never have loved you in the first place. The class system is a curse that the proud and selfish use to separate people from one another. We are all children of the one God. If my parents will not welcome you, then we will move somewhere else and make our own way. No one should separate what God has joined together. Let us simply trust in him.

So they went to the man of prayer and explained the whole situation to him. He gladly married them and sent them on their way with his blessing. They returned to the city, rented a small house and worked hard to earn their living. Even the richest people, with their palaces and worldly comforts, would envy the life of peace, love, and happiness that those young lovers enjoyed in their poverty. Along with their love for each other, they were also filled with the bliss of divine love. They gave themselves heart and soul in the service of God and he blessed them in every way.

karma • *bondage*

Seeker: Sadhu-ji, you say that it is our sinfulness that has broken our spiritual oneness with God. Why did God allow such evil to enter the world?

Sadhu: Apart from God nothing can be created, for God is the author of all that is. God is good and has created nothing harmful or detrimental, for that would be against his nature. Evil does not create, but only corrupts and perverts what God has created. Sin is not a part of God's creation. It has no independent existence. Sin is the delusive and destructive state of those who abandon truth and who, in irreverence, seek to satisfy their own selfish desires. We may think that we can obtain happiness by abandoning God's will and following our own whims and passions, but the result is not true happiness.

Think of light and darkness. Darkness is the absence of light. It is the same with sin: sin is the absence of what is good and true. Evil is terrible because people drive themselves to utter destruction—shipwrecked on the rocks for lack of a guiding light. For this reason, the Master who is light became God Incarnate. All who see his guiding light and follow the way it leads will safely pass through to the blessed haven where darkness is no more.

Seeker: But if God is almighty, why did he not create human beings so that they could not fall into the dark state of sin?

Sadhu: Sin arises because people deliberately violate God's order. Of course, God could prevent this by creating human beings differently. But then we would be like obedient puppets or machines, incapable of experiencing the bliss that can only be reached by freely choosing the good. Adam and Eve lived in sinless bliss, but they were free to choose God's will and direction or to follow their own appetites. Even Lucifer knew nothing of pride, a state that had never existed before he held himself to be God's equal. So through the choice of angels and human beings, sin arose. But God is almighty and can even transform evil into an opening for new and glorious ends. Firstly, God became incarnate to release us from the cycle of sin and death, thus revealing God's boundless, self-giving love in a way that would otherwise have remained unknown. Secondly, since we have tasted the bitterness and inevitable consequences of sin, we delight all the more in our release from its clutches – just as the sweetness of honey gives greater pleasure after the taste of bitterness. In unending unity with God, we are free to serve him with reverence and obedience.

Seeker: Modern philosophy, however, teaches that moral values are relative. They are products of history and culture. How then can one say that people are sinful?

Sadhu: It is said that a person suffering from jaundice sees everything with a yellow tint. People whose lives are colored by sin or guided only by the understanding of their minds also see reality colored by their own infirmity. When we shape and fashion spiritual truths according to our own ideas, it is not surprising if, in the end, we reject not only moral values, but also the reality of God. But the Master's work is to release seeking hearts from sin and death. He continues this work in the hearts of those who seek his help without regard to the opinion of others.

The blindness that sin brings about can be illustrated in many ways. Leprosy makes one's limbs numb and insensitive to pain and injury. People affected with this disease unwittingly receive wounds and allow the injuries to fester until the body is no longer able to survive. In the same way, sin deadens the heart and clouds the mind until people no longer have any sense of shame or disgust. Eventually, however, their eyes will be opened and they will see how sin has damaged and ravaged their souls; then there will be great sorrow and pain.

Many people are immersed in sin and don't even notice its great weight—just like a diver may be covered by tons of water without feeling its load. But if when the diver emerges from the water he tries to carry even a small bucket full, he will feel how heavy it is. The Master came to seek and save those who struggle with the burden of sin. He freely gives us rest and release from sin, but first we must feel the weight of it and turn to him for help.

People may not even be aware of their mortal danger. They are like the hunter who caught sight of a honeycomb on the branch of a tree overhanging a river. Catching sight of the honey, he forgot everything else and quickly climbed up. The honey was sweet and he was so enchanted by its flavor that he did not notice the alligators waiting in the stream below. Nor did he see that around the foot of the tree, wolves had gathered.

Worst of all, he didn't notice that the tree itself was infested with termites and was not strong enough to bear his weight. While he was still enjoying the honey, the tree fell and the hunter fell prey to the alligators. So too, the human spirit enjoys for a time the pleasant but fleeting delights of the senses, forgetting that the world is like a jungle fraught with dangers of every kind. Sin gnaws at the very foundation of our lives, threatening to fling us to our spiritual deaths.

The evil of this world lures us with clever words and beguiling enticements like certain snakes that fascinate small birds with their glittering eyes until they can devour them. Or think of the moth that gives no thought to the burning, destructive power of the fire. Fascinated by the flashing brilliance of the flame, it rushes to its own death. Likewise we often see only the allurements of the material world, seeking quick gratification of our own urges, and so rush headlong into spiritual death.

Once in the depth of winter, a bird of prey was busy feasting on a corpse that was floating toward a waterfall. When the bird came near the falls he wanted to leave the corpse and escape. But his claws were frozen to it and he could not fly away. He fell into the roaring waters and died a miserable death. Likewise, if we allow sin to numb our consciences, we become powerless to escape death and danger ahead, no matter how we struggle to escape.

By turning to the Master, however, and building our lives on him, we are saved from certain death and granted spiritual life that no one can take away. The Master frees us completely from the life-destroying seductions of this world. He sets our souls free from every bondage. Overcoming the attractions of the world, we mount on wings of prayer into the spiritual realms where our souls find peace in God's unfailing love.

Seeker: Has not Confucius said that those who respect the main principles of human conduct need not worry about their faults and lapses in smaller issues? They are excused. Why then do you say that all sin is dangerous, even dangerous enough to destroy our souls?

Sadhu: Not every organ in the body fails before the body dies. If the heart or brain fails, then life ends even if the other organs are healthy and strong. In the same way, the poisonous effect of one sin may destroy the spiritual life not only of a single soul, but also of a whole family or nation, even of the whole human race. Such was the sin of Adam. But remember, just as one word from the Master was enough to call the dead back to life, so one word is enough to restore spiritual life to those who have lost it.

If a wild animal or bird is tamed and then returns to the wild, its own kind may reject or even kill it, rather than accepting it as one of their own. They sense that long association with humans has affected its habits and manners. In the same way, the holy ones of the spiritual world cannot tolerate those who associate with evil and who have thereby corrupted their spiritual nature. Such people are alien intruders in the spiritual realm and they will not be at home there. Even in this world, sinful people despise and avoid the company of spiritual people. How then will they find joy in the eternal world of spirit? For them, heavenly bliss will be a living hell.

In this world, a traitor against king and country may escape punishment by seeking refuge in another country. But where shall we flee if we rebel against God? Wherever we go – in the physical or in the spiritual world – God is ever present. Our only refuge is to seek forgiveness and release from God.

Seeker: So is it true that, if we do not plead for mercy, God will send us to hell and punish us eternally for our sins? How is this perfect love?

Sadhu: Do not suppose that God casts sinners into hell. God is love and has no desire for anyone to suffer spiritual torment. But our own corrupt and sinful life deprives us of spiritual bliss. Heaven or hell is established in our souls and by our own choosing, long before our lives in this world come to an end. Sin is not an illusion or a fantasy. It is a real spiritual state. In this state, the human will separates itself from the divine and thus introduces the seeds of its own destruction.

God condemns no one to hell. No, it is we sinners who do the condemning. We condemn ourselves. Too many hearts are in a condition that they can only feel at home in hell—that is, outside the peace of the Master. God allows everyone to come to his kingdom. Indeed, he invites everyone most earnestly to come in, but if we prefer a life of sin, it is torture for us to stay there.

Pain and disease are not products of the imagination. They are all too real and we see how some diseases, like smallpox, can in a short time destroy the beauty of human skin, turning it into repulsive ugliness. Whoever longs to escape spiritual torment and death should therefore turn to the Master. He offers us release from sin and its consequences. His presence in our hearts and the influence of his Spirit rescue us from hell and lead us to eternal bliss as God's spiritual children.

moksa • *release*

Seeker: Sadhu-ji, you say that our sinfulness has separated us from God and yet our destiny is to live in oneness with him. How can we overcome the separation?

Sadhu: First, we must see that we have become unclean through our own sinfulness. We may try to cover this sinfulness with good works, but our good works are like dirty rags unless our hearts are cleansed first. When Adam and Eve ate of the forbidden fruit and were ashamed at their own nakedness, they tried to cover themselves with fig leaves. But fig leaves were too scanty a covering, so God gave them coats of skins to clothe themselves. Our attempts at good deeds are not enough to overcome our sinful inclinations. Nothing will protect us except the robes of righteousness the Master freely gives us.

Many of us have learned by bitter experience that our own efforts at goodness can give us neither peace of heart nor certainty of eternal happiness. When a rich young man approached the Master and asked how he might gain eternal life, he said, "Good Master!" and the Master rebuked him saying: "Why do you call me good? There is no one good except One." This young man had lived a devout life in accordance with religious law, but he lacked true peace of heart. The Master could see that he wanted to be good and upright, but he failed to recognize that the Master himself was the source of life. When the Master offered no rules or commandments and instead offered him the chance to give away all his possessions to the poor, to abandon his inner uncertainty and to enter into the Master's company, the man went away sad and unfulfilled.

If good works and religious observance had given the young man spiritual peace, he would not have sought out the Master in the first place. Not only did his moral efforts fail to give him peace, they hindered him from accepting the Master's offer. Not long afterward, an equally zealous man named Saul encountered the Master. Unlike the rich young man, Saul immediately left everything, gave up all he had and followed him. Everyone who ceases to trust in human goodness, and turns to the Master for release, shall receive true peace and spiritual life.

Seeker: Does God really forgive us for what we have done wrong? Is this what you mean by salvation or release?

Sadhu: God is love and forgives us freely. But God does even more than this. Forgiveness alone is not enough to release us from our sins. Complete release only comes when we are free from the urge to sin. It is completely possible for us to receive forgiveness and still die from the consequences of our sin. The Master came not only to announce our forgiveness, but also to deliver us from the disease of our sin, from its consequences and from death – to break the relentless cycle of sin and death.

Consider the man who suffered from a debilitating disease of the brain. At times it would cause him to act irrationally and unpredictably. Under the influence of one such attack, he unwittingly struck out and killed another man. At trial, he was sentenced to death. But when his relatives appealed for mercy and explained the medical reasons for his temporary insanity, the governor granted clemency and pardoned him. But before his friends and relatives reached the prison to share this good news, the man had died as a result of his illness. So he gained nothing from the governor's pardon. Quite apart from the pardon, he needed treatment for his disease. Only then might he have lived to enjoy his release.

It is treatment we need, not just forgiveness. In ancient times, religious law forbade people to drink the blood of animals or to eat certain foods. These customs undoubtedly arose from the belief that such foods caused certain illnesses or, perhaps, that they would foster some savage animal behaviour. The Master has said, "My flesh is food indeed and my blood is drink indeed," for they provide spiritual health and life.

Seeker: This teaching is hard. Who can accept it?

Sadhu: After the children of Israel fled slavery in Egypt, they lost faith in God and grumbled about all they had to endure. Things became much worse when they came to a place infested with poisonous snakes, where many were bitten and died. Then the people were sorry for their grumbling, and they asked Moses to pray to God for relief from the snakes. Moses prayed and was directed in a vision to make a snake of bronze and set it high on a pole. Anyone who was bitten had only to look upon the bronze snake, and the poison of the snakebite was made harmless.

Now, there were some who still grumbled and murmured, "If Moses would provide an antidote or some medicine against the poison, that we could believe, but what effect can a bronze snake have on real snake bites?" So in their unbelief, they refused to turn to the bronze snake, and they died. In the same way, the Master provides release from the deadly poison of sin if we turn to him in faith. Those who refuse to believe because they cannot understand the work of the Master with their minds will perish. But they will perish from the poison of their own unbelief.

Remember that the heart, not the head, is the temple of God. Spiritual and religious ideas are matters of the heart—not the head. If our hearts are filled with the presence of God, then our minds will also find enlightenment. Our physical eyes are useless, unless the light of day illuminates the world around us. Similarly, our minds and the eyes of our understanding are useless without the spiritual light of truth. The wisdom and understanding of the mind can easily be turned to clever instruments of evil if they are not subjected to the light of spiritual truth.

The Wise Men followed the star to Bethlehem. But when they reached Bethlehem, they no longer needed the star, for they had found the Master, the sun of righteousness. When the sun rises, stars lose their radiance. In India we have many genuine truth seekers who faithfully follow their star, but it is only starlight that guides them. In the Master we have the glory of the sun.

the prince and the thief

There was once a king who had a son. The prince was just and good, like his father. However, he knew nothing whatsoever of the condition of his people—how they lived and what they needed—because he lived in the palace and rarely saw any of the common people. So one day, he decided to live among them for a time and study their life so that he could help them when he became king. With his father's permission, he left the royal palace and lived among the people as an ordinary merchant. No one, except some of his courtiers, knew that he was the prince in disguise. Thus he lived and grew to know the lives of his people. He came to understand the ins and outs of their private and social lives and made plans and arrangements to serve them better.

As a merchant, he had to deal with all kinds of people, and he encountered all sorts and shades of characters. He was especially distressed to see how many people resorted to lies and frauds, selfishness and cruelty, theft and wickedness in order to make money for themselves. With his father's help, he often secretly aided the innocent victims of such unscrupulous characters. Nevertheless, he loved even those who had fallen into evil ways, and never injured those who deceived and maltreated him. He always forgave them and tried to help them change their ways. Many were reformed and became law-abiding citizens of his father's kingdom, although some did not.

Now, there was a thief who had so often injured innocent people and robbed them of their earnings, that the prince saw no option but to have him imprisoned. When the thief got out of jail, he wanted revenge against the prince whom he supposed to be an ordinary merchant. He entered the prince's hut to steal everything of value, but the prince overpowered him and admonished him for his shameful behavior: "You should work hard and earn your living in a respectable way," he told the thief. "If you needed anything, you should have spoken to me and I would not have refused your request. You disgrace yourself when you injure innocent people and steal their things. This is not right at all. You think that you are hurting others, but you are actually harming yourself. If you do not change your ways, you will surely come to grief on the judgment day. In hopes that you will see the folly of your ways, I forgive you this one last time. Do not mention this matter to anyone else, but use this chance that is given to you. You will not escape punishment the next time."

For some time, the thief kept himself in line. But after a few months, his old nature reared its ugly head again. One day, he set out to rob people in a distant village. Now in that village, there was a poor widow whose husband had died a year after their marriage. After his death she gave birth to a son. The sudden death of her dear husband was really a great shock to her and, sadly, she had no relatives or friends to aid her. But as she was a devout and God-fearing woman, she found peace and happiness in the worship and presence of her God, even in the midst of all her hardships.

Her son cheered her and helped her to forget the woes of the past. She raised him in the faith, fear, and love of God. She patiently endured all hardships and troubles, working very hard to make a living and to educate her son properly. In her need, she faced many trials and temptations and bravely overcame them all. At one point, when she was so poor that she could not provide milk for her son, some wicked young men tried to take advantage of her situation and lure her into immorality. But she watched and prayed, and through God's help, she remained faithful to what she knew was right.

In time, the widow's son grew to manhood and secured a good post in the city. He had to leave his dear mother behind in the village, but he faithfully sent her money every month. At the time of this story, the son had just returned to visit his mother after two years' absence. Embracing each other, their hearts overflowed with joy, and tears flowed from their eyes. It was a wonderful and moving scene. The son bowed in respect and honor at his mother's feet and put before her all the money he had saved for her to live out her days in comfort and security. The mother had also put aside some money every month from her small earnings for the day when her son would marry. Rejoicing in their long-awaited reunion, they placed these tokens of their mutual love in a purse, then ate and talked together for a long time.

Afterwards, they went to bed expecting to rise and see the next morning with joy and gratitude. But alas! No one knew that before the sun flashed in the eastern skies their tears of joy would turn into tears of sorrow and grief. For while the widow and her son were fast asleep the same thief, whom the prince had forgiven, broke into the hut searching for valuables. Just as he discovered the money in the purse, the widow and son awoke and discovered him. Thinking only of escaping with the purse, the thief attacked them with a sharp knife. What a tragic scene! The son lay dead on the floor in a pool of blood. The poor widow hardly noticed her own wounds. She screamed helplessly, fainted, and fell down on her son's dead body. Neighbors rushed to help, but they were bewildered and stunned to find the son dead and the mother lying senseless on top of him.

In the morning, the widow recovered a little from her swoon and three or four women helped her in the funeral procession, while the neighbors carried her son's coffin to the village cemetery. But as the coffin was laid in the grave, the mother fainted again. As the people tried to rouse her, they discovered that she had breathed her last. Killed by grief, she was buried with her son in the same grave. The entire kingdom was enraged at the news of this tragedy. A large reward was offered for the capture of the culprit. Some people suspected the thief, but no one had any evidence. Months passed without any progress in the case.

About this same time, the king became very ill and the prince returned to the palace to nurse his father. After some days, the old king died, and when news of his death reached the people, they lamented greatly. After the days of public mourning, the prince succeeded his father and was crowned king. On his coronation day, crowds of people had gathered from the four corners of his kingdom. Many of them were astonished to recognize the prince as the man who had lived among them as a merchant. During the reign of this new king, all the people prospered and the country progressed, because he knew his people well. He knew from his own experience how to deal with them and how to improve their condition.

Finally, the time came when wickedness should reap its evil harvest. One day, the thief was drinking and enjoying himself in a wine merchant's shop. That day he drank so much that he became senselessly drunk. He began to talk stupidly, and without realizing what he was saying, he confessed his guilt: "I killed the widow's son. With his money I enjoyed life. Now I defy any man who dares to catch me." He had hardly finished speaking when he was arrested and put in jail. After he came to his senses, he regretted his stupidity and unsuccessfully tried many tricks to escape his fate.

The next day he appeared in the court of a magistrate, but because of the seriousness of the offence, the magistrate sent his case to the king. As soon as the thief saw the king he turned white as a ghost. He knew it would be useless for him to try and talk his way out of anything, for he at once recognized the king as the merchant who had taken pity on him. The king asked him, "Do you recognize me?" "Yes, Your Majesty," the thief replied. Then the king asked further, "Do you wish to defend yourself?" "No, Your Majesty," he said. The king added: "Look here. I admonished you repeatedly, years ago, and had forgiven you. I gave you ample time to reform and become a good and law-abiding citizen. But you did not listen. You wasted all your precious opportunities and now your sin has found you out. Not only has your sin revealed you, but it also cries out against you and convicts you. Through your crime, you have determined your own fate." The thief was taken from the king's presence and executed.

In the same way, we will all be judged on the last day when God judges the living and the dead. The Master lived on earth as the son of man. He knows every one of us well. He cries out to us: "Now is the hour of pardon! Now is the day of salvation." If we are indifferent to a salvation as great as that now offered to us, our sins will surely convict us and lead us to death.

Seeker: Sadhu-ji, your teaching promises release from attachment to this world. Please tell me more about this spiritual freedom.

Sadhu: So many people are impressed by human ingenuity and our ability to tap the power of lightning, wind, light, and all the other myriad forces of nature. Yet, to overcome the passions and seductions of this world and to gain mastery over oneself is truly a much greater achievement. By leading a life of prayer, we receive from God the gift to dwell in the spiritual realm even while we remain in the material world. If we live in prayer, no force of evil or temptation can overcome us; we remain in safe communion with God without any fear. If we abandon the gift of prayer, we become like well-trained animals and no longer recognize our own imperfection, our relationship with God, or our responsibility for our neighbors.

Once the Master took three of his followers with him onto a mountain. There they experienced spiritual reality so intensely, that for a short time they saw something of the Master's divine glory. They were so captivated by that glimpse of the divine, they wanted to consecrate that place and remain there. How much more wonderful will it be when we enter fully into the spiritual realm and behold the unfading majesty of God.

Seeker: But isn't God everywhere? Can't we experience God by communing with nature and the world around us?

Sadhu: Both water and oil come from the earth. And though they are similar in many ways, they are opposites in their nature and their purpose. One extinguishes fire, the other gives fuel to the fire. Similarly, the world and its treasures are creations of God along with the soul and its thirst for spiritual truth. But if we try to quench the thirst of our soul with the wealth and pride and honors of this world, then it is like trying to extinguish fire with oil. The soul will only find peace and contentment in the One who created it along with its longing. When we turn to the living Master, we receive water that satisfies our soul. This water is a well of spiritual life that springs up deep within us.

It is pointless to seek peace in the things of this world. Peace and satisfaction are not to be found there. It is like the boy who found an onion and peeled away layer after layer, hoping to find something inside. When he had peeled away the innermost skin, he found nothing else. So this physical existence and all that it contains is empty and hollow until we discover the true source of peace. The water of life cannot be contained in earthen tanks, but those who approach the Risen One with a pure heart will find the answer.

Seeker: Are you saying that this material world is completely evil?

Sadhu: We must live in this world, and we can do so without losing our true spiritual nature. The things of this world need not harm us. Indeed, they can help us to grow spiritually. But this is only possible if we continually turn our hearts to the sun of righteousness.

Sometimes we come to a filthy, polluted place and find flowers blooming and giving off a sweet fragrance that overcomes even the stench around them. The plants are turned to the sun and receive its life-sustaining light. The filth does not harm them, but actually nourishes and mulches them so that they grow all the more richly. It is similar when we pray and turn our hearts to the sun of wholeness. We receive life-giving light and warmth so that our blossoming spiritual lives give off a gentle fragrance. Out of these gentle blossoms grow undying fruits.

When we neglect our spiritual life, then the same material things that are provided for our support become a poisonous curse. The sun provides light and warmth so that plants can grow and bloom, but the same sun withers and destroys the plant if its roots no longer draw in water. In the same way, air is a source of life and strength, but it is also the catalyst for rotting and decay. So watch and pray that you are rooted in life and not in death.

We all know that we cannot live without water. But while we need and use water, we must also watch that we do not slip beneath the surface. In the same way, we need the things of this material world, but we must exercise caution. God created earthly things for people to use. But we must not immerse ourselves in them or we will drown the breath of prayer and die.

Seeker: I cannot grasp what this means, to live in the world without immersing ourselves in it. Can you make this clearer?

Sadhu: Think of the ship; it belongs in the water, but water must not come into the ship – that would be disastrous. Similarly, it is right and fitting that we live in this world, and if we stay above the surface, then we can reach the safe harbor of life – and help others to do so. But it would be our demise if the world penetrated into our hearts. The spiritual person holds the heart free for the One who created it.

Waterfowl swim on the water, in constant contact with it, but when they fly, their feathers are free of water. So it is with those who pray: we live in constant contact with this material world, but when we rise in prayer, our spirits ascend into bliss without fault or blemish.

The creatures of the sea live their entire lives in salt water. Yet, when we taste their flesh, we find that it is not salty. It is the same with us. If we maintain an active prayer life, if we turn constantly to the source of life, we remain free of the world's corrupting influence.

Just as the bee gathers the sweet juice of the flowers and turns it into honey without harming their color or fragrance, so we gather in prayer the joys and benefits from all of creation. As the bees gather honey from various flowers and various places into the honey-comb, so we gather precious thoughts and experiences from every part of creation and, in communion with God, store them as honey of truth in our hearts. Then with boundless peace of spirit, we taste the honey wherever we are.

Seeker: As long as our souls are confined within material bodies, how can we ever really escape the corrupting influence of the material world?

Sadhu: The saltwater of the sea evaporates under the heat of the sun and rises into the sky. There it gathers into clouds and in time falls again to the earth, but now as sweet, refreshing rain. In rising from the sea, the water leaves behind all salt and impurity. So it is with our thoughts and desires in prayer. The sun of righteousness illuminates our souls and enables our thoughts and desires to rise up into the spiritual realm free from impurity. Then they return to us bringing refreshment and blessings to many.

Some plants close their leaves and flowers at sunset, opening up again with the gentle morning sunlight. They use the hours of daylight to take in the warmth and light, and this sustains them through the cold and dark of night. In the same way, if we open our hearts to the sun of righteousness, we are preserved even through the dangers and hardships of darkness, and we grow into the fullness and stature of the Master.

Some sea creatures have such a delicate structure that even the splash of a wave will tear them to shreds. They are so sensitive to the atmosphere around them, that if there is any hint of a change in the weather, they sink into the ocean depths beyond the reach of storms and waves. We, too, must be sensitive to the atmosphere around us. When the storm of evil and suffering threatens to tear us apart, we must dive at once into the ocean of God's love where there is eternal calm.

Seeker: Is it true then, beloved Sadhu, that one can experience miraculous protection through prayer?

Sadhu: I have experienced many dangers in my travels, often because intolerant people wished to see me come to harm. Once near Kailas, I asked directions to the nearest village. Out of spite, the villagers deliberately sent me down a dangerous jungle path. As night came on, I came to a river that blocked my path and there was still no village to be seen. Already in the dusk, I could hear the sounds of wild animals nearby. With no way to cross the river, I sat down and prayed, thinking that the end of my life was at hand. When I looked up, I saw a man on the other side of the river beside a fire. He called to me: "Do not be afraid! I am coming to help you." I was astonished to see him wade purposefully across the swift river. Coming up to me, he said, "Sit on my shoulders and have no fear." As easily as before, he walked straight across the current with me on his back. He set me down on the far bank, and as I walked beside him, both he and the fire disappeared.

Another evening, I was driven out of a village by an angry crowd, wielding clubs. They drove me into the forest until I came to a rock face and could go no further. There I huddled among the stones waiting for them to attack me and batter me to death. But nothing happened. After it was quiet for a time, I looked around and there was no sign of my tormentors. I built a fire, tended my wounds and slept at that same place. In the morning, I awoke to the sight of several men staring at me fearfully from a distance. Cautiously, they approached and offered me food and drink, asking, "Sadhu-ji, who were those men in shining robes who stood around you last night?"

Once, at a town called Rasar in Tibet, I was taken before the head Lama and accused of heresy because

I shared freely about the Master's work in freeing us from our sin. An angry mob dragged me to the edge of town, stripped me of all my clothes and cast me into a dry well that was then locked shut with a lid. My arm was injured in the fall, but worse than the pain was the smell. Many others had suffered the same fate and wherever I reached in the darkness I could feel bones and rotting flesh. The smell was vile. It was like hell. There I was tempted to doubt: "Where is the Master now? Why has he allowed this to happen?" But I also remember a sense of peace, a certainty that the Master was there with me.

I do not know how long I had been in the well, perhaps two or three days, when I heard a grating sound overhead. Someone was opening the lock and dragging away the lid. A rope came down and a voice commanded me to take hold of the rope. I grasped it with all my remaining strength and was dragged up into the night air. As I lay on the ground, breathing in the fresh air, I could hear the well being closed and locked again. When I looked around, I couldn't see anyone. I do not know who rescued me, but in my heart, I know that it was the Master.

The next day, I went again into the village and started to teach those who would listen. Some people dragged me again before the Lama, and I told him the whole story of my rescue. He was very angry and ordered that a search be made for the man who had taken the key to the lid. But when he discovered that the key still hung on his own belt, he was speechless. He ordered me to leave the village at once, lest my Master should punish him and the village.

Seeker: I find it difficult to believe that such amazing things are possible. Can we really move God through prayer to alter the natural course of events?

Sadhu: The scientific mind does not grasp how the author of life holds in his hands the created laws of nature. It is God who establishes the laws of nature. Thus, it is foolish to suggest that miracles violate the laws of nature. There are actually higher laws about which we know little or nothing. In prayer, we can come to gradually recognize these higher laws. Then, we understand that miracles are not only possible but even natural.

In very cold places, it is quite common for the surface of a river to freeze over while the water still flows beneath. I have crossed many such rivers safely and easily. But if I travel in tropical regions and tell people that there are bridges of solid water across flowing rivers and that I myself have walked across such bridges, then they shake their heads in complete bewilderment and argue that such a thing is impossible. Likewise, those who live only by the senses and by reason are utterly ignorant of the spiritual life and what things are possible through prayer.

God is spirit and God's ways are spiritual. Spiritual things cannot be grasped by human reason; they can only be seen with spiritual eyes. The greatest miracle is to be born in the spirit, to experience true peace. Once we personally experience the Master and how he has shattered the relentless cycle of sin and death and released us from our own sinful nature, we know that all things are possible with God. Once we have experienced this greatest of miracles, all other miracles seem small by comparison. That a poor, restless, impure, fallen soul can receive God's forgiveness and taste the Master's peace—this is the miracle of miracles. Whoever believes in this miracle believes in all miracles.

In great fear or anger or madness, a person can do extraordinary feats that seem far beyond human strength—like breaking iron chains. Clearly, this strength is latent within the human body and only comes to expression when the entire energy and concentration of mind and body is directed toward a single purpose. In meditation, our spiritual strength is similarly focused. Divine power flows through us, overcoming the chains of sin and spurring us to marvellous spiritual feats. But beware! Consider the power of guns and bombs that wreak destruction and devastation. Spiritual power can also be used for evil ends.

Seeker: God will truly grant whatever we pray for?

Sadhu: Some people think that we alter God's will and plans through prayer, but it is actually our hearts that are changed. The unfulfilled potential of our soul is ever striving to reach beyond the limitations of this imperfect life. When a bird first lays her eggs and begins to brood and warm them, there is only formless liquid inside. But as the mother continues to cover them with her own body, the liquid inside is transformed. It becomes solid and takes on the form of the mother. Similarly, our prayer does not change God. Rather, it is we who are transformed into the glory and image of God.

We do not pray to inform God of our needs. We pray in order to open our hearts to the giver of all blessings. When the Master departed from his disciples he did not pour the Spirit out onto them the same day. They needed a period of special inner preparation before they were ready for this gift. If we receive God's blessing without expecting it and without being inwardly prepared for it, we will appreciate neither the gift nor will we hold onto it for long. It was the same with Saul, the first king of Israel. He was not seeking to serve God, he was only concerned about lost donkeys. So when he received the spirit of God and was anointed as king, he was not inwardly prepared. Because of this, he soon lost both.

Seeker: What, then, is true prayer?

Sadhu: When we see a crane or heron standing motionless on the shore of a lake or pond, we might think it is meditating on the beauty of the water. But this is not so! The bird stands there for hours without moving, but as soon as it sees a frog or small fish, it darts forward and greedily snatches it. Many people have the same approach to prayer and meditation. Seated on the shore of the boundless ocean of God's love, they actually give no thought to his majesty or to the divine grace that cleanses us from sin and satisfies the hungry soul. Instead, they are consumed by the thought of receiving something for themselves, some morsel to gratify their self-indulgence. Having visited the very source of true peace and bliss, they fail to appreciate it and instead give themselves to fleeting pleasures.

The essence of prayer does not consist in asking for things, but in opening one's heart to God. Prayer is continual abandonment to God. It is the desire for God *himself*, the giver of life. Prayer is communion with God, receiving him who is the giver of all good gifts, living a life of fellowship with him. It is breathing and living in God.

A little child will run to his mother exclaiming: "Mother! Mother!" The child does not necessarily want anything in particular. He only wants to be near his mother, to sit on her lap, or to follow her about the house. The child longs for the sheer pleasure of being near her, talking to her, hearing her voice. This is what makes him happy. It is just the same with those who are truly God's children. They do not trouble themselves with asking for spiritual blessings. They only want to sit at the Master's feet, to be in living touch with him; then they are supremely content.

Climate affects the form, color, and growth patterns of plants and flowers. In the jungle we often see insects that have taken on the form and color of the grass and green leaves on which they feed. In the snow of the North, the polar bear's fur has the same snowy whiteness. The Bengal tiger wears stripes on its skin like the reeds where it lives. Our spiritual environment similarly affects us. If we remain in communion with God, our habits and disposition – even our appearance – are all changed. To pray means to be on speaking terms with God, to be in communion with him and to be transformed into his likeness. We begin to take on a glorious and incorruptible spiritual nature.

Seeker: Is the goal of prayer to lose our individuality and dissolve into oneness with God?

Sadhu: We have been created in the image of God. Our destiny is to be restored into that image. God came to us in the Master to restore us to God's divine nature. In this way, the Master transforms us into flames of spiritual fire. To become spiritual fire means to become like God. Even the smallest flame of fire is fire and has all the qualities of fire. This does not mean that our spirit is God's spirit, as some pantheists and philosophers suppose. We are not fragments of God's spirit. We are not God. God is distinct from us, but our souls can only find peace in oneness with God.

A sponge lies in the water and the water fills the sponge, but the water is not the sponge and the sponge is not the water. It is the same when I immerse myself in God. God fills my heart and I am in complete union with God, but I am not God and God is not I. We are distinct though not separate.

People are very different from one another—in character, temperament, and abilities—even though we are all created in the image of God. Indeed, if all the flowers in the world were of the same color and scent, the very face of the earth would lose its charm. When the sun's rays pass through colored glass, the color does not change, but the sun highlights and reveals its varied hues, its true charm. So the sun of righteousness shines through the varied characters of spiritual men and women, revealing God's boundless glory and love.

dhyanam • *contemplation*

Seeker: Sadhu-ji, some say that to encounter God we must fulfil some special devotional exercise of contemplation. What does contemplation really mean?

Sadhu: The wonderful peace and calm we experience in prayer does not come from our own thoughts or imaginations, but from the presence of God in our souls. The vapor rising from one small pond is not enough to form large rain clouds and drench the thirsty land. Such large clouds can only come from the mighty ocean. Peace cannot be found in our own subconscious minds, our own concentration, but only in the boundless ocean of God's love.

God is love and freely gives everything we need, both for our material and for our spiritual existence. But because the blessings of God's spirit are so freely given, we often take them for granted. If all people had open and receptive hearts, they could see and hear God's voice at all times and in all places. But we have lost this awareness. Through prayer, we learn to appreciate spiritual gifts, gifts that are at least as important for life as air and water, heat and light. Those who are focused on this material world foolishly waste the spiritual blessings offered to them, while those with a focused prayer life obtain true wisdom.

Dolphins can live in the deepest water without danger because they regularly come to the surface and take in the air that sustains them. We, too, must rise in prayer into the spiritual realm. To pray is to breathe in God's life-giving spirit that gives life and peace, even in this world.

The new-born child needs no instruction in drinking, but instinctively turns to its mother's breast for nourishment. For her part, the mother withholds no good gift from her child, but still the child cannot receive the mother's milk without effort. In the same way, we are carried at God's breast, but we must turn to God in prayer for the spiritual milk that sustains our souls.

The root tips of trees are so sensitive and responsive that they instinctively turn away from places where there is no nourishment and spread themselves instead in places where they can drink in moisture and life. I have seen green and fruitful trees standing in the middle of a dry and barren desert. These trees survive and flourish because their roots have driven down and discovered hidden streams of flowing water.

Some people live in the midst of evil and misery but still radiate joy and lead fruitful lives. Through prayer, the hidden roots of their faith have reached down to the source of living water. They draw from it energy and life to bear spiritual fruit. If we lead active lives of prayer, we will also gain the spiritual discernment to turn away from illusion and evil and to find the truth we need for life.

Seeker: You speak of discernment. Can you explain further what you mean?

Sadhu: Human consciousness is very subtle and sensitive. We can receive impressions from the unseen, spiritual world that express themselves in ideas and concepts familiar to us. Poets, artists, and musicians may experience these impressions in the form of rich colors, beautiful music, or other wonderful sights and sounds that come to expression in their artwork. Some people experience such things through dreams, some through visions, others during wakeful meditation. In prayer, light streams out from God, illuminating and guiding our innermost conscience. The discerning power of prayer enables us to distinguish the useful from the useless among such experiences. If we spend more time in meditation, we can recognize the relationship between the visible and invisible world ever more distinctly and clearly.

No thought, word, or deed is ever extinguished. They are forever imprinted on our souls—recorded in the book of life. Meditation provides the atmosphere for us to grow in fear and love of God so that these impressions are refined to contribute to our spiritual bliss. In meditation, the true condition of the soul is exposed, and God can reveal our failings in order to heal and bless us.

Seeker: Why doesn't everyone readily embrace this truth?

Sadhu: Once a woman was travelling along a mountain path carrying her child in her arms. The child caught sight of a pretty flower and lunged forward so unexpectedly from its mother's arms that it fell to its death on the rocks below. Isn't it clear that life and security were to be found at its mother's breast, not in the fascinating flowers? Many who set out seeking truth do the same thing. Catching sight of some fleeting and fascinating pleasure, they forget the spiritual milk God provides, an offering that comes with greater love than any mother can give, and they leap out into the world and are lost.

If we do not tend and care for a tree or a bush that bears good fruits or beautiful flowers, then it will grow wild and in the end it will be neither beautiful nor useful. It is the same with people of faith: if we neglect prayer and allow our spirits to grow sleepy, we will wither, fall back into our old evil ways, and die.

Once ten bridesmaids went out to meet the groom and lead the wedding procession. Five of them were wise and took extra oil in case he might be delayed. The others were foolish and took only their lamps. The groom was delayed in arriving, so the lamps burned low and the bridesmaids fell asleep. In the middle of the night they were awakened by the cry that the groom had arrived. They all rose, trimmed their lamps, and prepared to begin the procession, but the foolish ones noticed their oil was used up. They asked the wise ones for oil, but these knew there was not enough oil in their flasks to keep all ten lamps burning all the way to the banquet hall, so they told the foolish maids to go, awaken a merchant, and buy their own oil. They frantically tried to find someone to sell them some oil, but by that time the procession had arrived at the hall and the wedding feast had begun. The doors were locked, so the foolish bridesmaids missed the feast as well as the procession. Let us now follow the example of the wise maidens and fill the vessels of our hearts with oil of the Spirit. Otherwise, nothing will be left for us but grief and despair.

Seeker: What is this oil of the Spirit and how can I obtain it?

Sadhu: To obtain the blessings of a spiritual life, we must be ready to believe and obey without doubts and questions. Once the Master was in a temple where people were gathered for worship. Among the people was a man with a crippled and withered hand. The Master called to the man, "Stand up and come here to me." There the man stood in front of all the people, and the Master looked at him and said, "Stretch out your hand!" Without hesitating, the man held out his hand, and it was completely healed in that instant.

Imagine if the man had said: "If you are a prophet then you know my hand is withered and that I cannot lift it. First heal my hand and then I will be able to stretch it out." Or he might well have been embarrassed to put his hand on show in front of so many people and quickly run away in humiliation. Such reactions would have been reasonable and understandable, but the man's hand would not have been healed. Whoever wants to encounter God must be obedient. We must lift up in prayer our weak and withered hands, and then we will receive complete healing and new life – all our needs and longings will be fulfilled.

There was once a woman caught in adultery and brought by an angry crowd before the Master. Now, the law prescribed that she be stoned to death. Instead of addressing the crowd, the Master wrote quietly in the sand with his finger. Finally he lifted his head, looked at the crowd and said, "Let the one who has no guilt throw the first stone." Then he continued to write quietly in the sand. One by one the crowd dispersed – oldest to youngest – until only the accused woman was left. Then the Master lifted his head again, spoke to the woman and said: "If none of these people accuse you, then neither do I. Go, then, and lead a life pleasing to God."

With his finger, the Master had quietly written on the ground the sins and failings of each of those in the crowd who stood ready to condemn the woman, until each one left in shame and humility. With the same finger, he points to the secret wounds of sin in each person who seeks the truth. Then, with that same finger, he heals our wounds. As children hold a parent's finger to walk without falling, we, too, can grasp the Master's finger and walk securely the road to spiritual peace.

As the earth moves, we experience the changes of day to night and summer to winter. But with the sun, there is perpetual noon and perpetual summer. Likewise, the sun of righteousness is the same yesterday and today and forever. If we experience the exuberance of joy or the gloom of despair, it is only because our position shifts in relation to God. If we open our hearts in prayer and meditation, the warming rays of the sun are always there to heal the wounds of our sins and give us perfect spiritual health.

PARABLE

three seekers

The story is told of a wise man who met
three pilgrims on the road. The first was pale and withered and
cringing with fear. The wise man asked him, "Why are you in
such a frightful state?" Haltingly, the man answered: "All that
I have ever done wrong haunts me. I fear the consequences of
all the evil I have done knowingly or unknowingly. I am afraid
that I will suffer the eternal punishment of *naraka*, what men
call hell." The wise man spoke to him, saying: "It is sad and
distressing that you do not turn your heart and thoughts to
God, who alone is the source of all wisdom. Instead, you live
in continual fear of hell. So your pilgrimage is not genuine.
You are trying to offer your pilgrimage as a bribe to God, so
that you will not be punished for your sins. You will never find
peace along this path."

The second pilgrim was consumed with worries and doubts. The wise man asked him, "Why do you seem so sad and worried?" The pilgrim answered, "I desperately want to find the bliss and peace of the heavenly realm, but I fear I will not find it." The wise man rebuked him sharply, saying: "It is shameful that you fail to think of God's creative power and love. This alone should fill your heart with great awe and thankfulness. Instead, you are consumed by your own desire for peace and joy. You only pray in order to gain fulfillment of your own selfish desires. Such prayer is worthless and will never lead you to peace."

Afterward, the wise man turned to the third pilgrim who radiated joy and contentment. "Friend," he asked, "what is the secret of your joy and peace?" The pilgrim answered: "My heart is filled with joy, and I am filled with thankfulness to God who has opened the way for me to know his presence and find unity with him. May he open my heart more and more so that I can love and serve him with heart and soul and strength and so that I can worship him for love alone."

seva • *service*

Seeker: Sadhu-ji, your call to prayer and contemplation is compelling. Should everyone then abandon the distractions of the world to live the life of a hermit?

Sadhu: It is true that prayer is the means by which we experience the reality of God. But once God has become a living reality for us, we simply have to love our fellow men. We cannot do otherwise. Once we receive the new life of the Spirit, we begin to live in love. And living in love, we are moved quite naturally and joyfully to serve others. God is love and if we live in union with God, we have the strength and longing to love others. Service is a spiritual activity, the natural fruit of love. God, who is love, is ever serving and caring for Creation. Human beings are made to be like God and so they too should never tire of serving others.

Prayer without work is as bad as work without prayer. A broody hen satisfies its instinct by continuing to sit in some dark corner even after its eggs have been removed. So it is with those who remove themselves from the tasks of life and spend their time wholly in prayer. Such a life is as fruitless as the hen that sits on an empty nest.

Remember, there is a great difference between those who worship God with their lips only and those who do so with their hearts and lives. All too often, people pray to God in the name of the Master, but they do not really know him. They take God's name into their mouths and onto their lips but not into their hearts and lives. The Master guides us to recognize what will glorify God and benefit others. If we live in the Master and the Master lives in us, then our prayers bear fruit.

Once a man served his king with great faithfulness and courage and thus enjoyed the king's favor. But this man's son led a corrupt and selfish life. So when the son appeared before the king asking for some favor in the name of his father, the king replied, "Do not appeal to me in your father's name until you first go and live a life worthy of his example. Carry your father's honor in your heart, not only on your lips, and then I, too, will honor your request."

Anyone who has received help from another and yet is unwilling to offer help in turn is ungrateful and undeserving of any further help. Unless we offer all our gifts and abilities in service to God, who has given us life and breath and all we have, then we cannot expect to receive the spiritual help that God alone can give.

Seeker: We are weak and sinful—mere mortals. What help or service can we possibly render to God who is eternal and almighty?

Sadhu: God has no need of help from us. Our very existence is entirely dependent on God's constant help. However, if we offer ourselves in service, God blesses our efforts and adds his help.

When the Master approached Lazarus' tomb, his power and help was not needed to move the stone away. That was a task for others. Once they obeyed and removed the stone, however, then the Master did what was beyond human power: he called the dead man back to life. Afterward, there was still work left for others: they removed the burial clothes so that Lazarus could walk about in perfect freedom.

It is the same with those who are spiritually dead. We can roll away the tombstones of doubt and ignorance, but only God can breathe new life into them. Even then, they may still carry the burdens of bad habits and evil company, so we have the continuing duty to help free them from these entanglements. For this task, we must remain ever alert in heart and soul.

God often uses the least gifted people when some great service is needed. Why? Because people who know their own weakness are fully open to the power that God offers. When the Master fed the five thousand, he did not use his disciples. They were too full of doubt and worry, wanting to send the crowds away to fend for themselves. Instead, he turned to a small boy who had barely enough to feed himself. His mother had wrapped some barley cakes and dried fish for him, but he was completely willing to give all that he had in perfect trust that the Master would supply the rest. There may even have been wealthier people there with dried fruit and cakes of wheat, but they were not ready to give them up in such simple faith. So the Master fed the multitude with the simple food of a peasant boy.

Seeker: It requires such dedication to maintain an active prayer life. I do not see how one can find the strength to serve others as well.

Sadhu: The great gift of service is that it also helps the one who serves. Once when travelling in Tibet, I was crossing a high mountain pass with my Tibetan guide. The weather had suddenly turned bitterly cold, and my companion and I feared that we might not make it to the next village – still several miles away – before succumbing to the frost.

Suddenly, we stumbled upon a man who had slipped from the path and was lying in the snow. Looking more closely, I discovered that the man was still alive, though barely. "Come," I said to my companion, "help me try to bring this unfortunate man to safety." But my companion was upset and frightened for his life. He answered: "If we try to carry that man, none of us will ever reach the village. We will all freeze. Our only hope is to go on as quickly as possible, and that is what I intend to do. You will come with me if you value your life." Without another word and without looking back, he set off down the path.

I could not bring myself to abandon the helpless traveller while life remained in him, so I lifted him on my back and threw my blanket around us both as best I could. Slowly and painstakingly, I picked my way along the steep, slippery path with my heavy load. Soon it began to snow, and I could make out the way forward only with great difficulty.

How we made it, I do not know. But just as daylight was beginning to fade, the snow cleared and I could see houses a few hundred yards ahead. Near me, on the ground, I saw the frozen body of my guide. Nearly within shouting distance of the village, he had succumbed to the cold and died, while the unfortunate traveller and I made it to safety. The exertion of carrying him and the contact of our bodies had created enough heat to save us both. This is the way of service. No one can live without the help of others, and in helping others, we receive help ourselves.

Once two women appeared before the wise king Solomon. The first said: "Your Majesty! This woman and I live in the same house. I gave birth to a son, and three days later she also gave birth to a baby boy. But in that same night, her son died. So she sneaked up to my bed while I was still asleep, took my child from my side and left the body of her dead son in his place. In the morning, I could see that it was her baby, not mine."

At that, the second woman interrupted, saying it was not so. Then the two women began arguing in the presence of the king. The king called for silence and, to the astonishment of all present, he called for a guard to come with a sword, cut the living child in two, and give each woman half of the child's body. The second woman said, "So be it then!" But the first woman fell on her knees before the king and cried: "No, Your

Majesty! Have mercy and spare the child's life. Rather give him to the other woman." In those words, King Soloman recognized the true mother's heart and so ordered that the child be given to her.

Seeker: Your examples are full of hope, beloved Sadhu, but I am too selfish and sinful to be of any service.

Sadhu: There was once a convicted murderer who, instead of being hanged, was sent into battle with the armies of the king. He was gravely wounded, but he fought with bravery and valor and returned from the war a hero. The king, seeing his wounds and hearing the reports of his valor, not only pardoned him for his previous crime, but also rewarded him richly and gave him a position of honor in the kingdom. So it is in our spiritual lives. If we fight to save the lives of those oppressed under the weight of sin and selfishness, we will not only find forgiveness, but we will also enjoy spiritual bliss.

Some people are held back from serving others because they doubt their own abilities. They are like those recovering from a long illness. They receive nourishing food and rest and are no longer sick, but they remain weak and lethargic because they have not worked or exercised their muscles. We must simply set out in trust to bring the message of hope and faith to others. It is useless to take swimming lessons unless we are willing to enter the water and practice—first in the shallow water and then in the deep. In this way, we can gain strength and improve our technique. In order to help those who are struggling and sinking in the dark waters of inner need, we must enter the practical school of theology—prayer and spiritual union with God.

Seeker: Why share our spiritual blessings with others, when so often people only mock and ridicule us?

Sadhu: The Master said, "Resist not evil." Once there was a devoted Indian Christian who was praying in his house alone, when three thieves stealthily entered and took away all they could get. When the man had finished his prayers he noticed that all his goods were gone, except for the box over which he had been bowing in prayer. This box contained all his money and valuables. He immediately took the contents and ran after the thieves calling: "Wait! Wait! You have left some valuables behind. Perhaps you need these things more than I." When the thieves heard this, they thought it was a trap. But when they saw that he had no weapon and that he was alone, they came back to him. The man said to them: "Why didn't you tell me you needed these things? I would have gladly given you whatever you needed. Now, come home with me, and whatever you need you may have." The thieves, seeing the strange life of this man of prayer, were so struck that their lives changed forever.

If a blind man comes groping along the road, it is only right that we who can see should step aside and avoid bumping into him. And if he, by accident, bumps into us, we should not take offense, but rather help him find his way. If we get annoyed about it, it only proves that we are blinder than the blind man himself, completely lacking both common sense and human sympathy. Similarly, if anyone persecutes us because we follow the truth, we should—instead of being offended—forgive and pray for that person in love. If we continue to experience opposition, we lose nothing, since we experience it for the sake of the Master, the Truth, which is our reward.

If we serve in love, then our service will eventually bear fruit. If some people speak evil of us or hurl abuse and criticism, then we should love them all the more. They may yet taste the sweet fruits of our love.

When naughty boys see a tree with delicious fruit hanging heavy from its branches, they sometimes throw stones. But the tree does not respond by hurling stones back. Instead, it drops its delicious fruit for them to enjoy. The tree does not have stones to hurl, but it freely shares what it does have—the sweet fruit—without murmur or complaint. So do not be discouraged if some hurl abuse and criticism at you for following the spiritual life. It is a sign that they actually long for the fruit God has given you. And even if they attack you out of malice and spite, still you can offer spiritual fruits and reveal God's love.

A rebellious son once left his father's house and joined a band of robbers living along the road through the jungle. In time, he forgot his happy childhood and became as cruel and ruthless as the others. But his father never gave up hoping that one day he would abandon his evil ways and return home. In time, the father called his servants and asked them to go into the jungle, find his son, and tell him that his father was waiting to welcome him home and forgive him, if only he would abandon his evil ways. But the servants refused to go. They were afraid of the wild country and the fierce robbers.

Now, the man's older son loved his younger brother just as much as his father did. So, when no servant could be found to go, he set out himself into the jungle to find his brother and deliver his father's message. As he wandered through the jungle, the robbers spied him, attacked him, and wounded him to the point of death. Only then did his younger brother recognize him. Filled with grief and remorse at what he and his band had done, he embraced his dying brother and kissed him. With his last breath, the older brother was able to pass on the father's message: "Now my life's task and love's duty is done." So saying, he died in his brother's arms.

The young man was so moved by the loving sacrifice of his brother, that his heart was instantly changed. He abandoned his life as a robber, asked forgiveness of his father, and from that day on lived a new and upright life. When we think of how the Master died in agony to pass on to us God's message of love, should we then not also be ready to give our lives in bringing this message of hope to others?

Often, we can share the message of God's love more effectively by prayer than by preaching. Spiritual power emanates silently and unnoticed from those who pray and reveals spiritual truths to others, just as unseen radio waves from a powerful transmitter can convey messages to those attuned to them. In this way, a seeking person may receive the greatest help from someone praying alone.

The firefly with its flickering light and certain small plants in the Himalayas brighten the dark jungle as best they can. There are also tiny fish in the depths of the ocean that give light into that gloomy darkness. All the more should we be lights for all those souls wandering in the darkness of this world. Even if it involves risk or danger to ourselves, we should be eager to share our God-given light with those who are stumbling and in danger of losing their way.

Seeker: But if we give all our strength in serving others, how will we ever find time or energy to praise God?

Sadhu: God has no need of our praise. Does God lack anything that we mortals could provide? Those who seek to follow the spiritual life are like salt in the world. Salt crystals cannot give flavor to food unless they dissolve. If we dissolve the salt in a pot, it disappears but it does not cease to exist. Indeed, it can then give flavor to thousands of grains of rice.

It is the same with us. If we are not melted in the fire of love and spirit, if we do not sacrifice ourselves completely, then we cannot pass on to even a single soul the blissful experience of the spiritual life. If we do not sacrifice ourselves, then we are rather like Lot's wife who was turned to a lifeless pillar of salt. Yesu was melted in the Garden of Gethsemane and gave his life on the cross to open the gate of heaven for all. In the same spirit, we must be prepared to give up our own lives for the spiritual welfare of others. This is what will bring praise to God.

The sword of justice hangs threateningly even now over many souls. We must be willing to sacrifice our own desires – even our lives – for the benefit of those in danger of spiritual death. Then the world will recognize that true love abides in us and that we are children of the God who sacrifices himself for us.

Seeker: What happens if we fail to serve others?

Sadhu: If we repeat the same thought or word or deed over and over, then it becomes a habit. Habits determine our character. So we should carefully consider the consequences and implications of our habits. If we become indifferent to doing good, our capacity to do good will diminish. It is difficult to do something well. It is still more difficult to put right something we have done wrong. But it is altogether easy to destroy something. It takes great time and effort to grow a tree, but it is easy to cut it down. When it is dry and dead, it is impossible to bring it back to life.

If we do not make use of the spiritual faculties we have been given, then we will lose them. This has happened to certain fishes living in the deep waters of dark caves. They have lived so long in darkness that they have become completely blind. The same thing has happened to certain hermits I have met in the caves of Tibet. Therefore, do not let your spiritual sight grow dull, but make full use of all your spiritual faculties and strengthen them so that you are able to sense God's presence.

The pipe that carries fresh water is itself kept clean by the clear water that flows through it. In the same way, we are kept clean and pure if we allow God's spirit to constantly flow through us for the benefit of others.

There are many people who waste precious chances to serve God and their fellow human beings. They should rouse themselves and make full use of the time that is given to them. Once a hunter picked up some pretty stones by a river in the jungle. He used them to shoot at birds with his slingshot, and so one by one they disappeared into the water and were lost. Some time later, he was in a city and wandered through the market absent-mindedly tossing and catching the one stone he still had left. A jeweller caught sight of it, marvelled at such a precious gem and offered to buy it for several thousand rupees. When the hunter recognized the value of his stone, he cried out: "Woe is me! I have been carelessly shooting gems into the river. I could have been a millionaire. But thank God I have saved at least this one."

Every day of our lives is like a precious diamond. We may have wasted countless days already in idle and selfish pursuits, so that they are now lost in the depths of the past. But let us at least awake now, see the value of the days that remain and use them to acquire spiritual wealth. If we use them in selfless service to God and if we use them to warn others who are still frivolously throwing away their days in pursuit of fleeting pleasures, then we will gain the boundless treasure of heavenly bliss.

Seeker: Sadhu-ji, you speak much about the blessings of the spiritual life, but why do so much pain and suffering exist in the world?

Sadhu: It is difficult to understand the mystery of pain and suffering in the world. Ultimately, the root of suffering is found in sin, in separation from God. Still, God uses suffering to call us into the peace of his presence. If God could not use pain and suffering for our good, then he would not allow such things to remain in the world. The grain of wheat must lie in the dark womb of the earth before it can be called forth into the open air by the light and the warmth of the sun. Then it grows into a healthy plant and bears fruit.

Rain and windstorms wreak destruction, but they also cleanse the land of pests and disease. In the same way, the wind of the Spirit shakes us with its power, but its force brings spiritual health and blessings. Just as an earthquake can cause sweet springs to erupt in the desert making the land lush and fruitful, suffering can disrupt our lives and expose in our hearts springs of life-giving water. Then refreshing streams of thankfulness and joy flow where before there was complaining and grumbling.

When a bitter branch is grafted onto a sweet tree, both feel the knife and both suffer. But only in this way can the bitter tree bear sweet fruit. God himself suffered pain in order to introduce good into our evil nature. In this we see God's great love and in turn faithfully suffer the agonies of this world. We can then bear good fruit forever.

Seeker: So is suffering necessary for the spiritual life?

Sadhu: The divine order is established for our spiritual health and happiness. Remember that spiritual anguish and physical pain are not the same thing. Physical pain is the result of illness or injury, but spiritual anguish is the result of sin and separation from God. When we defy God and rebel against his divine order, spiritual anguish ensues. It is similar to the discomfort an Englishman experiences in tropical heat, or an Indian in the bitter cold. God does not prevent us from opposing him; instead he uses the resulting anguish to remind us that we are pilgrims and strangers in this world.

In the trenches dug during the First World War, flowers and fruit began to grow. Deep down the soil was richer and more fertile than on the surface. So it is when we suffer: the hidden riches of our soul come to light. Therefore, we must not despair when we see what appears to be a destructive process. This very process can set the hidden, unused powers of our soul to work.

The fruit inside the walnut is delightful, but the shell surrounding it is bitter. Suffering is unpleasant at first contact, but those who accept it for God's sake find within it the delight of spiritual peace. We do not attain real victory by escaping pain, but rather by discovering the grace to change pain into ease, death into life, and evil into good.

The silkworm struggles within the imprisonment of its cocoon, but this very struggle gives strength to its wings. If we open the cocoon and prematurely free the imprisoned creature, it will not have the strength for its new life and it will die. So God's children struggle in this world and in that struggle become strong and fit for the life that awaits them.

Our spiritual struggles in this world are a preparation for our eternal home. We can only really appreciate the blessings of comfort if we also experience the agony of affliction; the pleasure of sweetness, only when we taste the bitter; the value of the good, only when we encounter the evil; the worth of life, only when we pass through death. Misfortune and hardships in this life keep our spirits wakeful so that we do not abandon our true destiny and become comfortable in this fleeting world. When we have all reached a state of perfect spiritual health, suffering will end forever.

Seeker: Are you saying, then, that God deliberately inflicts suffering on us for our own good?

Sadhu: God has created everything in nature for a purpose, even if we cannot comprehend that purpose. Nearly every substance in nature that causes illness and death can also be used as healing medicine. We call them poisonous because we do not recognize their true qualities. In the same way, trials and afflictions can strengthen and deepen our spiritual lives if we make good use of them.

When we suffer, it may also benefit others in ways we can hardly imagine. By seeing our affliction and helping us, others may exercise their own spiritual gifts and grow toward perfection. God has no joy in our pain, but he sometimes uses pain and suffering as bitter medicines for the treatment of souls. If we turn against God and resist his help, then such trials become deadly poison to our souls.

If a newborn child does not cry out and scream, then it must be slapped until it does. No one has joy in slapping a child—only the longing that it makes full use of its lungs and draws in life-giving air. So in perfect love, God may strike us with blows and stings of pain so that the breath of prayer flows freely through the lungs of our souls. This is the only way we can become strong and fit for eternal life.

Look at the pearl. A pearl is a product of pain and suffering. Tormented by some foreign matter against its soft flesh, the oyster responds by embracing the irritant and transforming it into an object of great beauty. The creation of the pearl not only provides relief to the oyster but is also a source of wonder and pleasure to many others. But beware! The unique luster of the pearl can be easily destroyed. Ink or oils can contaminate and destroy its beauty. Pearls laid in ancient tombs often decay with the corpse of their owners; the dust of the pearls is then mingled with the dust of the dead.

Spiritual life—like the pearl—grows out of pain and suffering. And even when the pain has been transformed into a thing of beauty, the lustre of our spiritual lives can easily become contaminated and decay. We must continually watch and pray and turn to the Master with thankful hearts.

Thousands of years of heat and pressure come to bear on black carbon before it is transformed into a precious diamond. Even then, diamonds do not dazzle unless they have first been cut. When cut and polished, then the rays of the sun make them shine with wonderful colors. Scientists may manufacture artificial diamonds in laboratories, but careful examination exposes their inferiority. Likewise, we cannot attain spiritual perfection without passing through pain and suffering. We must live continually in the presence of God; then our trials will transform us into heavenly jewels, cut and polished by the Master's sure hand.

Seeker: Why do people laugh and ridicule those who choose the way of suffering?

Sadhu: Do not be surprised or distressed if others oppress and slander you. Light and darkness cannot exist together. People who are attached to their own desires and pleasures will always misunderstand and oppose the spiritually minded. Resisting any challenge to their own selfishness, they often become confrontational. Indeed, if you receive praise and compliments in this materialistic world, then beware that you have not abandoned the spiritual path altogether. Even if the unbelieving overcome their inclination to oppose you, this will only make it worse for you. Then they can begin to influence your spiritual life and hinder your progress.

Once there was a man who courageously confessed his faith and challenged people to abandon their selfish desires. Angered by the challenge of his life and words, his enemies took him and hung him upside-down from a tree. Even in this position, he had such peace of heart that he was not even conscious of the pain and disgrace. Turning to his tormentors, he said: "In this world, everything is upside-down and nothing is upright. You think you have turned me upside-down, but actually you have turned me rightside-up. I am like a transparency slide that casts its image correctly only when it is placed upside down in the projector. In your eyes I am upside-down, but in God's, I am forever upright."

Sometimes it is easier for the followers of God to die as martyrs than to daily give themselves as living sacrifices. We only experience physical death once, but if we faithfully follow God, we must die daily.

The Master needs living martyrs who offer themselves for the sake of others. All those who are ready to give up their lives in faithfulness to God—be it in physical death or daily service to others—will live with God forever in the fullness of joy.

Seeker: But surely, if selfish people despise us, we can at least depend on other spiritually minded people to stand by us.

Sadhu: Do not count on it! In order to rescue us, the Master renounced everything and was himself renounced by everyone. When he entered Jerusalem the people cried out with one voice: "Lord! Lord!" But within three days, they were so offended by his challenges to their comfortable and selfish lives that they cried with the same voice: "Crucify him! Crucify him!" To put your hopes on the support of other people is to build your house on sand. Today they will praise you and build you up, but tomorrow they will cast you down so that no trace remains.

Do not feel sorry for yourself even if those who lead spiritual lives turn against you. If you faithfully follow the leading of God's spirit, God and the hosts of the heavenly realm will stand by you. You should not get discouraged. The time will soon come when God will reward the unselfish love of the faithful.

Seeker: It often seems that those who are faithful to God and who seek the truth must suffer while others enjoy comfort and ease.

Sadhu: In the bitter cold of winter the trees stand bare and seem to be dead. But in the spring, they burst forth into leaf and flower, and the first fruits begin to appear. So it was with the Master's death and resurrection. So it is with all of us who faithfully bear the burden of suffering and death. Though we may seem crushed and dead, we will yet bear beautiful flowers and glorious fruits of eternal life.

Do not be jealous of those who lead a comfortable life. It is possible for sheep to wander away from the fold and find good grass along the edges of the jungle. However, they are actually in great danger, and in the end wild animals will tear them to pieces. By contrast, those who stay with the flock may appear feeble and the grass may be less green, but there they are safe under the shepherd's watchful eye. It is the same with the followers of God; those living in comfort and success do not necessarily enjoy his blessing.

Whether we like it or not, we will encounter suffering and danger in our lives. If we do not bear the cross of the Master, we will have to bear the cross of the world — with all its earthly goods. Those who bear the Master's cross know from experience that this cross bears them and takes them safely to their destiny. But the cross of this world actually drags us down and leads to destruction. Which cross have you taken up? Pause and consider.

The snake and the silkworm begin their lives with similar bodies. But as they grow, the snake remains a snake no matter how many times it sheds its skin, while the silkworm casts off its ugly form and emerges from its cocoon as a completely new creature, flying on the air with delicate wings. So the believer casts off this material body and enters into spiritual bliss, soaring forever in the heavenly realm while the sinner remains a sinner even after death.

The Master opened the gates of heaven for all who follow in faith. As soon as we follow in his footsteps, accepting in faith the way of suffering, we begin to experience unbounded joy. Only those who believe can understand and accept this joy. Heaven is closed to unbelief. God gives an enduring joy and deep happiness even in the midst of pain. This joy can uphold us in the midst of suffering and lead us through the open gate of heaven.

Seeker: You speak of the Master — God incarnate — suffering. How is such a thing possible?

Sadhu: The body and the spirit are distinct, yet they are so finely interwoven that the spirit is aware of even the slightest injury to the body. So the Creator is distinct from his creation, but wherever people experience pain and grief, God himself feels it.

A clean person cannot stand being in a filthy place even for a short time. Those who live in communion with God find it very unpleasant to live among ungodly people. Indeed, some abandon the world to live as hermits in the desert or in caves. If we, as sinful people, cannot stand the company of evildoers, what agony must the Master have known. When we speak of his suffering, we often mean the six hours of the crucifixion. But his whole life as the embodiment of holiness among the defiled must have been a trial. He took this on himself to rescue us from death. It is beyond our comprehension. Even the angels cannot comprehend it. It is an amazing thing that God, out of love, should become one of us that we might gain eternal life.

Once, as I traveled through the Himalayas, there was a great forest fire. Everyone was frantically trying to fight the fire, but I noticed a group of men standing and looking up into a tree that was about to go up in flames. When I asked them what they were looking at, they pointed up at a nest full of young birds. Above it, the mother bird was circling wildly in the air and calling out warnings to her young ones. There was nothing she or we could do, and soon the flames started climbing up the branches.

As the nest caught fire, we were all amazed to see how the mother bird reacted. Instead of flying away from the flames, she flew down and settled on the nest, covering her little ones with her wings. The next moment, she and her nestlings were burnt to ashes. None of us could believe our eyes. I turned to those standing by and said: "We have witnessed a truly marvelous thing. God created that bird with such love and devotion, that she gave her life trying to protect her young. If her small heart was so full of love, how unfathomable must be the love of her Creator. That is the love that brought him down from heaven to become man. That is the love that made him suffer a painful death for our sake."

God, who himself suffered anguish in this world, is able to protect and rescue those who suffer now. He gives relief when the time is right. Nebuchadnezzar threw three young men into the furnace, but God was with them, and its raging fire could not harm them. God is with all those who have received new spiritual life. They pass through the fires of physical pain and affliction and dwell in the peace and safety of God's presence.

the king and the farmer

Once there was a good and just king who
loved his subjects and wanted to do everything he could to
help them. At times, he would wander about his kingdom
disguised as a commoner in order to learn more about their
difficulties and troubles. In this way, he hoped to find ways to
help them.

On one such journey he met an old man who was driving
his oxen into a field and struggling with a heavy burden on his
back. It pained the king's heart to see such a thing, so he went
to the man and said: "Come, Grandfather, can I not help you?
Give me your bundle and I will carry it to the field for you." The
startled old man looked up from beneath his load. He dropped
the sack to the ground, took a deep breath, and replied, "You

are very kind, my son, but I am poor and have no way to repay such kindness."

The king quickly reassured him: "Don't worry about that, Grandfather! It will be ample repayment if I can remove from my heart the pain of seeing you toil under such a heavy load." Saying this, he picked up the sack, threw it over his shoulders and went with the old man and his oxen. When they reached the field, the old man thanked him profusely and asked: "What is your name, kind sir, and where is your home?" The king sat down beside the man and did not answer at first. He was not used to such heavy work and he had to catch his breath. After a short rest, they spoke together.

King: Why do you ask my name and where I am from? I do not want any reward for my service. But you, how can it be that you still work so hard in your old age?

Farmer, in tears: What can I say? It would be better for me to remain silent. My heart aches to think about my misfortunes, to remember all that I have lost.

King: What do you mean? Please tell me. My heart goes out to you, and perhaps I can help in some small way. Please tell me what has happened.

Farmer: I cannot think what good can come of telling you my tragic story, but since you insist, I will tell you. I am very poor. I had two sons, and in my old age I depended on them very much. Last year there was a terrible famine in our land, and it hit us very hard as we were already poor. I sent one of my sons to the nearest market town–some miles from our village–to buy wheat. Alas, my second son also went with him to help him. When they arrived, they went to a big grain merchant, purchased the wheat we needed, and at once left to return home.

While they had been bargaining with the merchant, another man watched from some distance away. As it turned out, this man was a robber and a bitter enemy of the grain merchant. Apparently, the merchant had given evidence against him years before, and he had been sent to prison. So after his release, he was always looking for a chance to take revenge.

After my sons left the shop, this robber saw that the grain merchant was alone. He attacked him, murdered him, and ran away with all his money. A short time later, one of the servants of the murdered merchant arrived and found his Master dead in a pool of blood. He immediately cried for help, and a large number of people hurried to see what was the matter. The police also arrived and immediately arrested the poor servant.

Of course, the servant told the police how a few moments before he had seen a couple of young men with his master.

Judging by their dress and accent, he assumed they were from our part of the country and had come to buy grain. Shortly afterward, he returned and found to his great distress that his master had been brutally murdered and that the murderers had run away with all the money in the shop. The servant urged the police to go after the two men and arrest them. As soon as he told his story, the police sent a contingent of five men after my sons. They quickly caught them and took them back to the shop where they had purchased wheat.

Being quite innocent and ignorant of all that had happened, my sons went with them quite willingly. They hoped to ask the merchant to testify on their behalf that they were not thieves or robbers, but simple, honest villagers who had purchased grain at his shop. They had neither weapons nor bloodstains nor any of the stolen money.

When they returned with the policemen and saw the awful scene, they were dumbfounded. Never in their lives had they seen anything so horrible, and they couldn't even utter a word. So most of the people standing around assumed they were the culprits, although a few more experienced and educated men said that it was rather a sign of innocence. But the cruel policemen would not listen to these cautions. They beat my sons mercilessly, and my eldest son was so badly injured from the blows that he fell unconscious. His clothes were stained with blood from his own wounds.

As soon as I heard this terrible news, I left my oxen and goods with a neighbor and hurried to the town where it had happened. When I arrived, I went straight to the government officials and with great humility and deference, I begged them to have pity on me and my sons. But they raged against me, treating me harshly and ordering my arrest as well, saying: "Are you so blind and stupid, old man, that you do not see the merchant's blood all over your sons' clothes? Do you not hear how his blood cries out for justice?" So you see, dear friend, how blind our government is and how cruel are the police. People cry out for justice, but there is no justice. The cruel and wicked prosper while the poor and innocent suffer terribly.

Well, after cursing and threatening me, they finally let me go, but they beat my sons again and dragged them to court where they were to be tried. My poor sons said repeatedly that they knew nothing of what had happened and that they were innocent, but their words fell on deaf ears. The police twisted the facts and fabricated evidence against both my sons to show that my elder son had killed the merchant and that his younger brother had been an accomplice. On the basis of this false evidence, they were both found guilty. My elder son was sentenced to death, and the younger sentenced to seven years hard labor. I wept bitterly and cried for justice, but who listens to the pleas of the poor?

A few days later, the robber who had actually murdered the grain merchant, attacked and killed another shopkeeper. This time there were many witnesses so he could not escape. He was tried and sentenced to death, and when he realized that his own death was inevitable, he confessed to the murder of the merchant as well.

On hearing the dying man's confession, the magistrate sent two officers to the prison with orders that my sons should be released. But alas, my elder son had already been hanged, and the younger had died from despair and from the wounds he had received in custody. After burying my two sons – the joy of my life and my comfort in old age – I returned home broken-hearted and weak.

King: Your story breaks my heart, Grandfather. It is more than a man can bear. Why did you not appeal to the king for justice?

Farmer: My dear sir, I tried everything I could, but the government officials would not permit me to approach the king or appeal to him. In the end, I had no choice but to drink the bitter cup of sorrow and tribulation. Our king is good and kind-hearted, but his officials are cruel and they

wisdom of the sadhu

do not tell His Majesty the whole truth. I hear that our gracious king sometimes goes about in disguise to discover the needs and woes of his subjects and to alleviate their suffering, but I do not know if it is true. So what cannot be cured must be endured.

King: Indeed, what has been done cannot be undone. I will help you if I can, but no sorrow or worrying will bring back your sons. Sooner or later, all of us leave this world. But tell me more about your life and your neighbors.

Farmer: Kind sir, there are some who weep and some who sing. Usually, each man's home is his castle. From what I have seen, the rich are no happier than the poor, nor are the poor less satisfied than the rich. Indeed, those ridden with worries and needs are less content than the poor. Before this awful misfortune, I was as happy as the king in his palace. Even now I try to willingly accept my fate and live as happily as I can. Truly blessed are those whose hearts know the peace of God; otherwise, the poor and the rich, the beggar and the king are all alike.

King: Would it give you pleasure, Grandfather, if the king invited you to live in his palace?

Farmer: Is the king's palace safe from sorrow, suffering, and death? There is more pleasure in one's own simple hut with a simple meal after a hard day's work than in the luxuries of a palace. In fact, my sufferings have taught me so many valuable lessons, lessons that were unknown to me before. I am happy wherever God places me. The death of my sons was almost more than my heart could bear, but now I am convinced that the separation is only temporary. My days are also numbered, and one day I will also cross the river of death.

Today, I will scatter these grains of wheat on the field; in a few days' time they will begin to decay, but then new grains will grow. In the same way, all of us will die, but our souls will grow into a new form. Our mortal bodies will decay, but our souls will rise to dwell in eternal bliss with the Creator where there shall be no more death nor sorrow nor pain.

King: Grandfather, you have more than repaid me for my small service. Your words have been a greater help to me than any help I have given you. It is now I who must offer you thanks. Where have you found this divine knowledge?

Farmer: When I was suffering so greatly, a man of God visited me. He sympathized with me but also helped me spiritually and instructed me in divine truths. He told me that just as our dear king goes about among his people to help them, so also the heavenly king wandered the earth to better know the condition of his people. He, too, helped, instructed and comforted them. And in the end, he showed the depth of his love by sacrificing his own life for their sake. Ever since I accepted the truth taught by this holy man, I have found new peace and thankfulness for all I experience.

King: It gives me great joy to hear of this peace you have found. But I must not keep you any longer from your work. Perhaps I will have the pleasure to call on you again sometime.

Saying this, the king took leave of the farmer and went on his way. The farmer, of course, had no idea that the man with whom he had spoken was actually the king in disguise. When the king returned to his palace, he investigated the man's story and found every word of it to be true. He ordered severe punishment for the policemen involved, as a lesson to others. Then the farmer received a summons to the palace, where the king received him with honor and affection and granted him a generous pension so that he could live out his days in comfort and ease. Greatly amazed, the farmer returned to his home, praising the kindness and justice of God and of the king.

amrita • *eternity*

Seeker: Sadhu-ji, you say that one day all suffering will cease and that we will enjoy eternal unity with God. What can you tell me about our eternal home?

Sadhu: We are never satisfied with one thing for long. We always want to change our circumstances and environment. This restlessness stems from our deep inner awareness that the fleeting things of this world can never satisfy our souls, can never give us a sense of stable and unchanging fulfillment. Only when we turn to the Master will our desires be transformed, and perfect peace, the gift no one tires of, will reveal itself as the deepest longing of our hearts — indeed, the soul's only quest.

There are many unhappy people who rejoice in the thought of entering heaven after death, yet who do not realize that heaven must begin here on earth. How will they ever enjoy being in a place to which they are not accustomed? I see so many people, even among the devout, who cannot live together in harmony during this short earthly life. How will they ever live together during the whole of eternity? I do not believe in a religion that offers a heaven only after this life is done. It is true that our dwelling place is not here; our real home is elsewhere. But many of those who wait for heaven will find the spiritual realm strange and not at all to their liking.

In the spiritual realm, heaven and hell are two opposite states of being. These states develop already now within each person's heart. We cannot see these two states of the soul any more than we can see the soul itself. But we can experience them just as clearly as we can feel physical pain or taste the delicious flavor of a sweet fruit.

The injury caused by a physical blow may fester and worsen until it causes tremendous pain or even death. And we know that fruit may nourish and sustain us beyond the mere enjoyment of its sweet taste. Similarly, each sinful act carries with it painful consequences, just as each good deed carries with it wholesome consequences. Though we may not yet fully perceive the pain or pleasure of those consequences, we will when we wholly enter the spiritual realm.

Sometimes we experience a sudden sensation of spiritual peace or pain, something that comes to us from the spiritual world without any thought or desire of our own. This sensation is the beginning of heaven or hell. It may recur and vary, but gradually one or the other prevails according to our spiritual orientation. By repeatedly fostering one or the other, we determine our spiritual destiny. So the foundations of heaven or hell are laid within our hearts long before we pass on to the next world. When our life in this world ends, we enter into whichever spiritual state our desires or passions have prepared.

Seeker: If we ourselves choose our eternal destiny, then surely no one would choose eternal death, would they?

Sadhu: God has indeed created the human heart with an inclination to accept his living Spirit. But many have developed such love and devotion to material things that their hearts are unable to turn to spiritual things. Think of the charcoal. It has a natural inclination to receive fire within itself, but without oxygen the fire cannot enter it. If we drown ourselves in worldly distractions, the living fire cannot be kindled and we remain in darkness. Only if we turn to the Master will the temple of our hearts be cleansed. Only then will we be ready to accept his spirit into our hearts. Only then can we experience true bliss and lasting peace.

The fitness of our hearts and thoughts to receive God's spirit is like that of violin strings. If they are properly tuned, in harmony with one another, then the touch of the bow produces beautiful music. If not, then there is only discord. Whenever our hearts are truly ready to receive God's spirit, they will produce heavenly airs and joyous harmonies—both in this life and in the spiritual world.

When the Master gave his own life on the cross, there were two thieves executed beside him. To all appearances, the three men suffered the same fate, but from a spiritual perspective there was a vast difference. One remained cynical and irreverent, even mocking the Master as he suffered. The other thief felt deep pangs of remorse and recognized the great injustice of the Master's execution. Opening his heart thus in love and in union with the Master, he heard the comforting words that he would that same day enter paradise. Paradise does not only exist beyond the grave; it already begins in the human heart. Some glorify the womb of Mary that housed God Incarnate.

This pales in comparison to any heart into which the Master is invited, transforming it into heaven itself.

Once in a vision I saw a man arrive in the spirit world. He was in great distress, for in all his life he had never given a thought to anything but earning his daily bread. At the same time I saw another man die and enter the spirit world. He was a doubter, obstinate in his opinions. In love and compassion, saints and angels met both of them and tried to guide them toward the heavenly light. But again and again they turned back toward the shadows, because sin had so warped them that they doubted and discounted everything. As I watched, I wondered what their end would be. One of the holy ones turned to me and said, "God may yet have mercy on them."

Then I saw another man enter the world of spirits. He had led an evil life. When the angels and saints went to help him, he cursed and reviled them, saying: "God is altogether unjust. He has prepared heaven for such flattering slaves as you and then casts the rest of us into hell. And you call him Love!" Just then the magnificent voice of a high angel called out, saying, "God gives this man permission to enter heaven." Eagerly the man stepped forward. When he reached the door of heaven, however, and saw the holy, resplendent palace with all its glorious inhabitants, he began to feel uneasy. The angels encouraged him to go a little further to see the Master sitting on his throne. But when he did, the light of the Sun of Righteousness revealed the impurity of his sin-defiled life. He turned away in an agony of self-loathing and fled in such haste, that he cast himself headlong into the bottomless pit.

Then I heard the voice of the Master saying: "Look, my dear child! I forbid no one to enter my kingdom. No one forbade this man, nor did anyone ask him to leave. It was he, with his impure life, that fled this holy place. Except you be born of the spirit, you cannot see the kingdom of God."

Seeker: Is eternal bliss available to everyone?

Sadhu: Many long for it, but miss it through their own foolishness. Once a poor beggar sat for twenty-one years on top of a buried treasure without knowing it. He burned so hotly with desire for money that he even hoarded the pennies he received. Yet, he finally died in utter poverty. Because the greedy man sat so long in that one spot, a rumor arose that he had hidden something valuable there. So the governor had the place excavated and the hidden treasure chest was found, filled with precious gems. The greedy beggar died in ignorance of the wealth that lay a few inches under him, and in the end the riches went instead into the royal treasury. God's promise of bliss is very near to us—in our mouths and in our hearts.

Many have died of thirst though surrounded by the ocean. Its salty water simply could not quench their thirst. Just so, there are many people who live in the midst of God's boundless love, but die of thirst because sin has turned the sweet water of God's love into bitterness for them. Those who turn away from sin and seek spiritual life from the Master find fountains of living water arising from that sea of love. They find full satisfaction and enduring peace. This is heaven.

Once a faithful follower of the Master was tortured until he was at the point of death. But he was filled with such spiritual joy that he turned to his tormentors and said, "Oh, that I could open my heart to you and show you the wonderful peace I have found." Amazed at his inner peace in the face of such suffering, those foolish people tore out his heart hoping to find something precious inside it. Of course, they found nothing. The reality of heavenly bliss is known only to those who open their own hearts and accept it.

Occasionally our sense of inner peace and spiritual bliss fades. This may be because of some disobedience or because the Spirit departs from us for a time so that we recognize anew how empty and restless our souls are without God. In this way, God can reveal again to us our utter weakness and teach us that without spiritual life we are nothing but dry bones. God wants to protect us from the pride and complacency of thinking that we have achieved something out of our own human strength. God trains and educates us so that we turn ever anew to the Master and so find never-ending spiritual happiness.

Sometimes those who are filled with God's spirit are overwhelmed by divine bliss and fall into a state of faintness or even unconsciousness. This is a reminder that flesh and blood cannot inherit the glories and blessings of the spirit world. Only when our souls are set free from these mortal bodies shall we experience the fullness of spiritual peace where pain and suffering, sorrow and sighing, woe and death cease forever.

In the midst of polar ice fields, one can find flowing streams of hot water. In the same way we can find, even in the midst of this loveless and sorrowful world, restful streams of heavenly peace. It happens wherever the fire of God's spirit glows within human hearts.

a warning to the west

Christian: Sadhu-ji, you have personally experienced Yesu to be the Master who leads us to inner peace and salvation. Don't we have an obligation to bring this truth to heathen peoples everywhere?

Sadhu: We must break the old habit of calling people of other faiths "heathen." The worst "heathen" are among us. We should love people of other faiths, even agnostics and atheists, as brothers and sisters. We need not love everything they believe and do, but we must love them.

Even an idolater worshipping a stone may experience something of God's peace. This does not mean that there is any consoling power in the stone, but for some, it may be a means of concentrating their attention on God. God grants to all people peace in accordance with their faith. The danger, of course, is that the worshipper will not advance spiritually, and will become more and more attached to the material object rather than to the living God—ultimately becoming as lifeless as the stone. Such a person will no longer be able to recognize the author of life who alone can fulfil the longing of our hearts.

Christian: But don't we have an obligation to profess our faith and share it with others? You yourself heard about the Master from missionaries who went to India.

Sadhu: When we have really encountered the Master and experienced release from sin, then sheer joy impels us to share it with others. We cannot sit silent about what God has done; we must give witness to it. Anyone who has experienced the Master's peace — whether man or woman, boy or girl, rich or poor, laborer or farmer, writer or priest, judge or official, doctor or lawyer, teacher or pupil, government official or missionary — he or she is only a follower of the Master to the extent that they witness to the truth. But bearing witness does not necessarily mean preaching in the market or from a pulpit. We have opportunities of giving witness to the Master wherever we are. We can do this through an upright life, a blameless character, through integrity of behavior, by our enthusiasm, and by our love for the Master, sharing with others what he has done for us. Every person, not only with words but with his life, can be a witness for the Master.

A Sufi mystic was on a journey. He had with him a quantity of wheat. After being on the road for several days he opened his bags and found a number of ants in them. He sat down and pondered over their plight. Being overcome with pity for the little lost creatures, he retraced his steps and returned them safely to their original home.

It is amazing how we humans can show so much sympathy to such little creatures. How then is it possible to lack sympathy and fellow feeling in our dealing with one another? Many have gone very far astray and do not know the way back. Surely it is our duty to guide the lost back to the way of righteousness and to help them find their eternal home.

There are many people in India and around the world who would like to hear about the Master. These people need witnesses to the truth but not Western culture. Indians desperately need the Water of Life, but they do not want it in European vessels! The Master chose simple fisherman as his followers because he had a simple message, not a philosophy. The world has enough of teaching and philosophy.

Christian: Haven't you visited America and western Europe? What did you think of our Christian witness and heritage?

Sadhu: What homesickness I had in Europe! I felt like a bird in a cage. The whole atmosphere was heavy for me. Many people thought I suffered from the cold climate, but this was not so. I have experienced far greater cold in the Himalayas. It was not the physical atmosphere that oppressed me, but the spiritual atmosphere.

In India, one feels everywhere – even through idols and altars, pilgrims and penitents, temples and tanks – that there is a desire for higher things. In the West, however, everything points to armed force, great power, and material things. It is this power of evil that makes me so sad. India is more and more seeking the Master's truth. The West is in danger of becoming more and more indifferent. And yet the West owes so many of its blessings to Christianity. At one time the ostrich could fly, but because the ostrich stopped using its wings, it became unable to fly. So are the people of Europe and America – they do not appreciate the faith of their forebears and are fast losing it.

The West is like Judas Iscariot, who ate with Yesu, only to later deny him. The West ought to fear the fate of Judas, lest it hang itself on the tree of learning. You have so many privileges. We in the East have to give up many things when we become Christians. For you, it is not so. Therefore be careful that you don't lose your only possibility for eternal happiness. I am reminded of the hunter who was pursued by a tiger. He had no fear because his hut was nearby and he was sure that he had the key in his pocket. On reaching it, however, the key was gone, and although there was only the thickness of the door between him and safety, he was lost.

Once when I was in the Himalayas, I was sitting upon the bank of a river; I drew out of the water a beautiful, hard, round stone and smashed it. The inside was quite dry. The stone had been lying a long time in the water, but the water had not penetrated the stone. It is just like that with the "Christian" people of the West. They have for centuries been surrounded by Christianity, entirely steeped in its blessings, but the Master's truth has not penetrated them. Christianity is not at fault; the reason lies rather in the hardness of their hearts. Materialism and intellectualism have made their hearts hard. So I am not surprised that many people in the West do not understand what Christianity really is.

Many modern thinkers in the West do not believe in the miracles of our Master. To my mind, it's already a miracle that there are still spiritual people in the West at all. In America, for example, one sees a good deal of Christianity, but it does not address the spiritual needs of the people. Just as salty seawater cannot quench thirst, much of American religion cannot satisfy a spiritually thirsty person because it is saturated with materialism. The Master's words, "Come unto me all who are heavy laden and I will give you rest," are true as regards the East, but I think that for America, he would say, "Come unto me all who are heavy gold-laden and I will give you rest."

Looking at the motto "In God We Trust" on the American dollar one might think the Americans are very religious people, but the motto should read, "In the dollar we trust." Americans are seeking the almighty dollar, not the Almighty God.

Although America is a "Christian" nation and there are many sincere Christians in America, the majority of the people there have no faith. There, where it is so easy to have religion, where religion is offered on every side and no one is persecuted for their beliefs, life should be peaceful. Instead, there is a mad rush and hustle and bustle after money and comfort and pleasure. In India, many Christians suffer bitter persecution but continue to find happiness in their new faith. Because it is so easy to have faith in America, people do not appreciate what a comfort there is in faith.

Christian: What advice do you have, Sadhu-ji, for Christian churches in the West?

Sadhu: A scientist had a bird in his hand. He wanted to find out in what part of the bird's body its life was and what the life itself was. So he began dissecting the bird. The result was that the very life of which he was in search mysteriously vanished. Those who try to understand the inner life merely intellectually will meet with a similar failure. The life they are looking for will only vanish.

When I returned from Europe, I began reading the writings of the German mystic Jakob Boehme and was attracted to him as soon as I had read the first two or three pages. This simple, uneducated shoemaker had an experience of God that has influenced millions of people. I may be wrong, but I am more and more convinced that simple people like Boehme have a pure intuition and grasp easily and readily the Master's profound spiritual truths. Educated people, especially those I met in the West, repress their native intuition and substitute in its place a kind of artificial rationalism. That is why the Master called simple fishermen as his disciples.

I studied theology in a theological seminary. I learned many useful and interesting things no doubt, but they were not of much spiritual profit. There were discussions about sects, about Yesu Christ and many other interesting things, but I found the reality, the spirit of all these things, only at the Master's feet. When I spent hours at his feet in prayer, then I found enlightenment, and God taught me so many things that I cannot express them even in my own language. Sit at the Master's feet in prayer; it is the greatest theological college in this world. We know about theology, but he is the source of theology itself. He explains in a few seconds a truth that has taken years to understand. Whatever I have learned has been learned only at his feet. Not only learning, but life, I have found at his feet in prayer.

I do not condemn theologians wholesale, but it is unfortunately the fashion in Western thinking to doubt and deny everything. I protest this tendency. I never advise anyone to consult theologians, because all too often they have completely lost all sense of spiritual reality. They can explain Greek words and all that, but they spend too much time among their books and not enough time with the Master in prayer. It is not that I oppose all education, but education without life is certainly dangerous. You must stop examining spiritual truths like dry bones! You must break open the bones and take in the life-giving marrow.

seeker and master

Once upon a time, there was a rich man who enjoyed a life of luxury. But, unhappily, he had no son. He used to say to his friends and wife, "Oh, pray for me that God may mercifully grant me a son who will inherit my property and keep up the name and fame of my family." After some time, God answered his prayer and gave him a beautiful and promising boy.

His parents entertained many plans for their newborn. Their expectation and hopes knew no bounds. When he was six years old, his father arranged for him to have the best possible education, which continued until the age of fifteen. He was also trained in all the skills and responsibilities of manhood.

At the age of eighteen, he married and the young couple began to lead an exemplary family life that was the envy of everyone who knew them. Blessed with peace and plenty, they enjoyed all the pleasures of the world and knew nothing of woe or worry. But some months after their marriage, the young man's parents, whom he loved so much, died of cholera. While he was grieving over the loss of his parents, thieves broke into his house and carried away all his money and valuables, leaving the couple destitute. Prosperity makes friends and adversity tests them, so one by one all his "friends" deserted him.

He could not help exclaiming in despair: "Oh, what shall I do and where shall I go? We are expecting a child, but alas! I shall not rejoice as my dear parents did at my birth, nor shall I be able to do as much for the child as my parents did for me. Oh, how fickle is fate!" His good wife comforted him, wiped his tears with her tender hands, and said: "My dear husband, don't weep and worry. Trust in God. Whatever he has done, he has done well; and whatever he may yet do, it will no doubt be for the best. Do not lose heart."

In time, the child was born into these adverse circumstances. The man nursed and attended to his wife and child as best he could, but unhappily, the child died after a few hours. In tears, the man went to bury the little body and, on his return home, found his wife unconscious. Unable to revive her, he held her head in his lap. After a short time, his wife opened her eyes. They looked at each other lovingly but could not speak. The husband was exhausted from grief and bereavement, and the wife was weak from the difficult birth. After a time, her eyes closed forever.

The shock was more than the young husband could bear. He collapsed, unconscious, and God only knows how long he remained senseless on the ground. One of his neighbors happened to pass that way and discovered all that had happened. He immediately went and called friends and acquaintances in the neighborhood. They all came and arranged for the funeral of his dear departed wife.

At the graveside the young man stood, weeping bitterly, and cried out: "Oh, that I myself and all my sorrows and sufferings could have been buried in this grave instead of my dear wife! My dearest friend and companion, my beloved, has departed leaving me all alone. Alas! How can I bear such misfortune!" With that, he fainted again and fell to the ground. This heart-rending sight moved to tears all who were there. They gently lifted him up and carried him home. After he had rested, they tried to console him, saying: "What is done is done. It is useless for you to grieve any more. Sooner or later, we all have to leave this world, every one in his or her own turn."

Grappling with the death of his loved ones, the man began to think more and more about spiritual things. After some time, he went to a spiritual teacher to find inner peace. But nothing brought comfort or peace into his distress. In time, he went into the jungle and began to live alone as a hermit in a cave. He prayed earnestly to God: "O my Creator and Master, have pity on me, a miserable sinner! Either take me away from this world or grant me a glimpse of your truth, so that I may find new life." For days, the man waited and prayed constantly to God, and at last his prayer was answered.

Early one morning, a man approached his cave. Seeing the newcomer approaching, the man thought to himself: "Perhaps, like me, this man has suffered much, is now weary of this world, and is wandering about in search of some shelter and peace. Or maybe he is some traveler who has lost his way." When the man reached the cave, he greeted the brokenhearted hermit with great affection and sympathy. The hermit rose with respect, spread a blanket on the ground, and invited the stranger to sit down.

Hermit: May I have the pleasure of knowing your name, honored stranger, and may I ask where you have come from and what brings you to this lonely spot?

Stranger: You cannot understand the meaning and significance of my name. I am the shepherd and have come down from on high to seek and save my lost sheep.

Though the hermit did not fully understand his remarks, the stranger's personality and words made a deep and wonderful impression on him. It was as if, for a moment, his black heart were illuminated by the stranger's glorious and shining presence. He felt as if he himself was the lost sheep and that the shepherd had come to help him. He had a great longing to know the stranger better.

Hermit: For how long have you been on this errand?

Stranger: Since the beginning.

Hermit: I can see that you must be a prophet. Please tell me more about yourself, bless me, and make me your disciple.

Stranger: I was and I am and I will be. I have been called God-with-us, the Holy One, the Prince of Peace and the King of Kings. I appear to those who seek me, and in the fullness of time I came as the Anointed One to bring release from sin. Now I have come as the Shepherd in answer to your prayer. I have come to give you peace.

Hermit: O, my God and Master, today I have found the author of life. Now I care nothing about my earthly losses, because I have received everything. From now on, I am your child and your servant. You are everything to me. Why did you remain hidden from me for so long?

Stranger: Until now, you were not ready to see me as you see me now. But in reality, I have always been with you. You rejoice to see me sitting beside you, but it is more important that you recognize my presence in your heart and soul. Even your hardships have prepared you to know me better. These trials have expanded your heart and made you aware of your own need for inner peace. Only by coming to the end of your own strength, did you finally turn in faith to God for help.

Hermit: O, how happy I am! My whole being longs to praise you and give thanks to you, my Master. But more than the praise of my lips, I know that you desire inner gratitude, a heart open to the overflowing joy of your presence. Forgive me, Master, if I dare to ask you one more question. How do I know that what I now experience is real and not some product of my imagination?

Stranger: My son, do not try to grasp spiritual truth with your mind. Many say that spiritual experiences are subjective or imaginary, but it is not so. What you experience is real. You have sought long to open your inner eyes and ears to eternal truth. Have I not promised that if you seek, you shall find? Rejoice, then, that your prayers have been answered and you can believe because you have seen me. All the more should those rejoice who believe even though they have not seen me as you have.

Hermit: O Master, I long to be your true and faithful servant. Grant that I may never lose the blessing I have received today. Protect me from doubts or indifference, and give me grace that I may be faithful to the end.

Stranger: When we stand on the edge of a precipice and look down, we feel dizzy and are afraid. The depth may be only a few hundred feet. But when we gaze at the heavens, though our eyes may range over much greater heights, we are never afraid. Why? Because we cannot fall upwards. When we look up to God we feel that we are safe in him and that there is no danger whatsoever. But if we turn our faces away from him, we are filled with terror lest we fall from reality and be broken to pieces.

Always watch and pray. Never mind if you lose your earthly wealth. This has to happen sooner or later. Now you have real wealth that no one can ever take away from you. Indeed, be grateful if the loss of your earthly riches and honor empties your heart and makes room for real and abiding treasures. Remember I am with you always.

In reverence and gratitude, the hermit bowed down at the feet of his Master. Looking up, he saw that the stranger had vanished. From that day forth, he gave himself, heart and soul, in service to the Master.

When Sundar Singh disappeared in the Himalayas in 1929, the world mourned. His twenty-three-year pilgrimage as a sadhu—a wandering, penniless pilgrim—had led him through at least twenty countries on four continents. He had profoundly influenced tens of thousands of people. Indeed, in the first half of the last century, no spiritual teacher from the East was better known.

Sundar Singh was born on September 3, 1889, in Rampur, a village in the Punjab, and educated at the Presbyterian missionary school nearby. It was there that he burned his Bible on December 16, 1904. He experienced a conversion the following year (after which his family threw him out of the house and disinherited him) and was baptized at St. Thomas Church, Simla, on September 3, 1905. Thirty-three days after that he took on the ascetic lifestyle of a sadhu.

His real significance does not lie in place-names and dates, however, but rather in the devotion and selflessness with which he spread the Gospel, and in the sincerity with which he lived what he preached. As German scholar Friedrich Heiler once put it, "He is India's ideal of the disciple of Christ – a barefooted itinerant preacher with burning love in his heart. In him Christianity and Hinduism meet, and the Christian faith stands forth, not as something foreign, but like a flower which blossoms on an Indian stem."

———

Sundar Singh's spirituality is best approached against the backdrop of his religious upbringing; it grew out of an intense struggle to come to terms with key elements of both his ancestral (Sikh) faith and his adopted one. Despite his father's fierce opposition to Christianity, which he saw as the religion of India's colonial oppressors, Sundar Singh's desire to serve his new master, Yesu (Jesus), in fact led him to fulfill his deceased mother's dream that he would one day choose the way of the sadhu.

Recognized by their traditional yellow robes and ascetic lifestyle, Indian sadhus (literally "poor man" or "beggar") forsake creature comforts to live lives of devotion and prayer. Some become hermits, while others wander from place to place as spiritual teachers;

still others practice penance through mortification, lying on a bed of nails or walking through fire.

Throughout India, devout people consider the way of the itinerant sadhu – as its Buddhist and Muslim counterparts, the *bhiksu and fakir* – to be the highest form of religious devotion, so much so that sadhus are generally welcome in every village. Unlike priests and other formal religious leaders, they can move freely among all castes and are even permitted in women's quarters, which are otherwise off-limits to men.

Throughout his life Sundar Singh maintained the highest respect for the familiar expressions of devotion he had grown up with – Hindu and Buddhist, Sikh and Muslim. Still, the intense, mystical encounter that had led to his conversion left him forever changed and gave him an unwavering dedication to Christ. Thus, although he never criticized any religious practice that was sincerely observed, he was always ready to relate how Yesu had touched and transformed him. For him, Yesu was the Truth – the completion and fulfillment of the deepest human longings for inward and outward peace, and it was unthinkable to keep it to himself. It was for this reason alone that he wandered for months and even years at a time across the Indian subcontinent, braving the elements and enduring the attacks of anti-Christians.

As a sadhu, Sundar Singh found a ready welcome in most of the places he stayed, though reactions varied when it was discovered that he was a follower of Yesu. (Christian sadhus had professed their faith in India for hundreds of years – ever since the time of the Apostle Thomas, who supposedly founded the first church there – but they were always an unpopular minority.) Particularly on his journeys into Tibet, he was attacked by violent fanatics. It was there (probably in 1912), that he was arrested, tossed into a dry well, and left to die – but later rescued by a mysterious stranger.

———————

After years of traveling in India, Tibet, and Nepal, Sundar Singh set his sights further afield. In 1919 he journeyed to China, Malaysia, and Japan; in 1920 he toured Australia, England, and the United States, and in 1922 he traveled throughout Europe, holding public addresses in Geneva, Oxford, London, and Paris, and numerous other cities in Germany, Holland, Sweden, Norway, and Denmark. Everywhere he went, large audiences and prominent leaders – religious and secular alike – received him enthusiastically. In many countries he visited, special trains were organized to transport tens of thousands of listeners to the cathedrals and sports arenas where he spoke. The emergence of a more tolerant liberalism in Christian theology explains part of his widespread appeal; on the other hand, many Europeans were simply curious to see a "real" Eastern mystic firsthand, especially one whose very manner and appearance evoked traditional images of Jesus. There was also his reputation as a miracle worker—something he worked tirelessly to dispel. More than anything else, however, it was Sundar Singh's understatedly simple faith and authentic practice of Christ's teachings—something utterly out of sync with western materialistic intellectualism—that his audiences found so compelling.

Admonished for his lack of familiarity with twentieth century science, Sundar Singh said, "What is science?" "Natural selection, you know, and the survival of the fittest," he was told. "Ah," Sundar Singh replied, "but I am more interested in divine selection, and the survival of the unfit." Then there was his attitude to money. Sundar Singh refused to accept it, even when he needed it, and when someone forced a gift on him he gave it away. There was also his unorthodox attitude to matters such as church membership, of which he said:

I belong to the body of Christ...to the true church, which cannot be understood as a building of tiles and stones. It is a body of true Christians, living and dead, visible and invisible. But I have nothing against anyone becoming a member of an organized church...As for the Apostolic Succession, I don't believe in it, though if this belief helps people in their spiritual life, then let them believe in it...But if the living Christ is really near us and lives in our hearts, why should we reject him – the kernel of our faith – and cling to a dried-up outer shell?

Inevitably, such views, which endeared him to the masses, drew criticism from ecclesiastical authorities and even to open hostility in certain quarters. Completely disregarding (or failing to comprehend) the mystical character of his teachings, influential theologians attacked Sundar Singh's teachings as incompatible with traditional Christian dogma. A few attacked his character as well, suggesting that he was little more than a charlatan and publicity seeker, which in turn led friends and supporters to defend his reputation.

———

A flurry of books and articles appeared from both camps. Perhaps not surprisingly, the most intense debate took place in heady halls of German academia, where the controversy became known as the *Sadhustreit* ("sadhu fight").

After some time the *Sadhustreit* died from lack of interest. The whole debate had, of course, been largely incomprehensible to those who looked to the Sadhu for inspiration. But insofar as it exposed the fundamental antagonism between western rationalism and eastern mysticism, it served a purpose. It confirmed Sundar Singh's own suspicion that while western Christianity might be rich in organization, theology, doctrine, and tradition, it was poor in spirit and sorely needed re-centering on the foundation from which it had strayed: the living Christ.

———

During the last few years of his life, as his health failed, Sundar Singh published six slim books. He wrote them at the urging of friends and followers (the first in his native tongue, Urdu; the rest in English), but he could not have foreseen the overwhelming demand that arose for them once they were published. Within the space of a few years, all six volumes had been translated into every major Western language; into Japanese, Chinese, and other Asian languages;

and into every principal dialect of the subcontinent. This collection is drawn almost entirely from those books, and from transcripts of addresses delivered at large public gatherings.

Despite Sundar Singh's considerable written legacy, however, it is important to remember that he was not an author at heart, and that his home was neither the writing desk nor the speaker's podium. By all accounts, his public addresses—like his writings—were most commonly noted for their disappointing brevity. Sundar Singh found his true home on the dusty roads of the Punjab, along the narrow tracks through the Himalayas, in the villages where his listeners gathered to drink in the peace of his deep, dark eyes, and in the relaxed cadences of quiet conversation. Finally, his home was in Christ, the one to whom he turned both detractor and flatterer alike, and from whom—as this concluding anecdote from one of his European translators shows—he drew inspiration for every word and deed:

> The Sadhu was very reluctant to speak about himself; he was always concerned that no one be distracted from Christ. I had an unforgettable experience in this connection. We were on a train, and the pastor traveling with us told the Sadhu that at the meeting we were to attend that evening, he wanted to introduce him to an important guest—a woman who could not find peace, although

she had gone to hear many famous Christian speakers and sought their advice. The Sadhu remained quiet for a while and then, addressing the pastor, asked him almost brusquely not to introduce him to the woman. The pastor seemed offended, but though he kept quiet the Sadhu noted his displeasure. So he explained, "Dear pastor, this lady has something to learn, but she would not learn it if I met with her. She must learn it from Christ, and he is much nearer to her—and will mean so much more to her—than any man."

sources

The Christian Witness of Sadhu Sundar Singh: A Collection of his Writings, edited by T. Dayanandan Francis (CLS, Madras, 1989). The comprehensive collection of all published writings of Sundar Singh along with various previously unpublished materials and an extensive biographical introduction. Available from the publisher at cls.org.in.

Sundar Singh: A Biography, by A. J. Appasamy (Lutterworth, London, 1958). The definitive biography of Sundar Singh, rich in detail and written from a critical-scholarly angle. The Indian edition (in English) can be ordered from CLS at the address above.

Sadhu Sundar Singh: A Personal Memoir, by C. F. Andrews (Hodder & Stoughton, London, 1934). Reflections by a close friend of Sundar Singh.

The Gospel of Sadhu Sundar Singh, by Friedrich Heiler (ISPCK, Delhi, 1996). An English translation of Heiler's comprehensive study, which first appeared in German in 1924. Heiler offers a fascinating overview of the Sadhu's life and teachings, and analyzes them with respect to other strains of religious mysticism, both in the East, and in the Christian tradition.

Sadhu Sundar Singh, by Phyllis Thompson (O. M. Publishing, Bromley, UK, 1992). The most extensive biography currently in print outside of India. Though this book lacks the references and critical analysis offered by Appasamy, it is eminently readable and includes the essential details of his life story.

other titles from plough

THE GOSPEL IN DOSTOYEVSKY
Fyodor Dostoyevsky
A powerful collection of passages from the novels of a man
whose gift for illustrating the social implications of the Gospels
remains unmatched.

SEEKING PEACE
Johann Christoph Arnold
Where can we find peace of heart and mind – with ourselves,
with others, and with God? Arnold draws on the wisdom of some
exceptional (and some very ordinary) people who have found
peace in surprising places.

PROVOCATIONS
Spiritual Writings of Kierkegaard
Søren Kierkegaard
An unparalleled introduction to the cantankerously witty Dane,
brimming with parables, sayings, and essays that, among other
things, attack the "mediocre shell" of conventional Christianity.

FREEDOM FROM SINFUL THOUGHTS
Johann Heinrich Arnold
Pastoral advice on finding freedom and wholeness in a world full
of distractions and temptations.

Plough Publishing House
Walden NY, USA
Robertsbridge, East Sussex, UK
Elsmore, NSW, Australia
www.plough.com